HOME-SPUN FUN
Family Home Evenings

Gospel Basics

Lessons and Activities for All Ages
with Memorable Thought Treats

Gospel Basics

Articles of Faith	Baptism	Beatitudes	Child of God
Faith	Fasting	Forgiveness	Honesty
Obedience	Prayer	Priesthood	Repentance	Sabbath Day
Sacrament	Testimony	Tithing	Word of Wisdom

Covenant Communications, Inc.
American Fork, Utah

Printed in the United States of America
Fourth Printing: May 2001

Home-spun Fun Family Home Evenings—Gospel Basics

ISBN 1-57734-143-0

HOME-SPUN FUN
Family Home Evenings

Your family can always have fun while learning the gospel of Jesus Christ with these home-spun fun activities. With these visuals you can create interesting lessons, scripture posters, activities, and treats. Week after week, children and parents will look forward to being together as you learn and share these gospel basics. As you do so, you will learn to become an eternal family and to live the gospel.

Each home-spun fun activity is designed to teach gospel principles. Children will remember lessons taught if they can create their own visuals. Simply photocopy activities on colored cardstock paper, then get out the watercolor markers or crayons, scissors, glue, and other simple supplies.

We offer ideas from the sources listed below to enhance your family home evenings. First, search the scriptures using the SCRIPTURE LESSON ideas. Then use the specific references to the following books published by The Church of Jesus Christ of Latter-day Saints. Add these to your family home evening library. All books are available at the Church Distribution Center in Salt Lake City, Utah, or at LDS bookstores.

- □ Family Home Evening Resource Book
- □ Children's Songbook
- □ Book of Mormon Reader, New and Old Testament, and D&C Stories
- □ Primary manuals: Nursery - Age 3, Ages 4-7, and Ages 8-11
- □ Gospel Principles
- □ Uniform System for Teaching the Gospel (Missionary Discussions #1-6)

MISSION POSSIBLE! Symbol: Many of the family home evening lessons have the "MISSION POSSIBLE!" symbol (shown left). These are areas of focus for future missionaries. See missionary discussion reference at the bottom of each lesson.

How to Use This Book

1. **DISPLAY** the Heart-to-Heart Family Home Evening Chart (patterns follow this page) to assign tasks and remind family members of family home evening. Read 1 Nephi 17:15.

2. **PLAN** your family home evening each week with the Heart-to-Heart Family Home Evening Chart. Copy and color chart and hearts, adding family names. Laminate and attach hearts to chart with sticky-back Velcro or tape, assigning a new task each week. Plans: Activity, lesson, scripture, music, prayers, and treat.

3. **COPY** the home-spun fun activities several weeks ahead and obtain supplies.

4. **PURCHASE** and prepare Thought Treats to match lesson activity.

5. **DISPLAY** Bite-size Memorize poster each week in a frame where the whole family can learn (sliding in a new poster each week).

6. **ENJOY** these home-spun fun activities to create loving family ties.

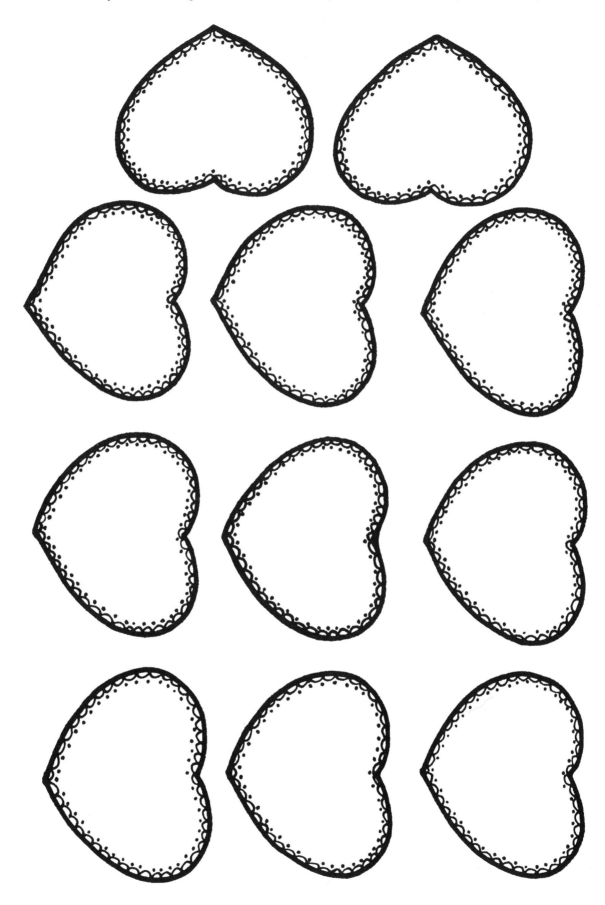

TABLE OF CONTENTS

HOME-SPUN FUN   *Family Home Evenings*

Activity Preview for Lessons #1-17 (continued on next page)

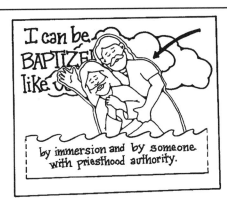

ARTICLES OF FAITH: Testimony Builders (13 Lucky Numbers game) 2, 4

BAPTISM Like Jesus (immersion 3-D pull-up card) 6, 9

BAPTISM Into Jesus Christ's Church (Promises picture word poster) 6, 10

BAPTISM: Accountability (Annabelle the "udderly" responsible cow) 6, 11

BAPTISM Promises (I Promise and Heavenly Father Promises puzzle) . 7, 12

BAPTISM (Waters of Mormon scripture word search) 7, 13

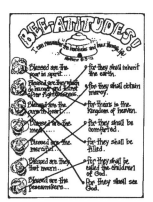

BEATITUDES: How to Get to Heaven ("Bee"-atitude cross match) 14, 17

BEATITUDES: How to Be Happy ("Bee"-atitude Blessing wheel)   15, 18

BEATITUDES: Have a Good "Bee"-atitude (match puzzle) 15, 19

BEATITUDE Blessings ("Bee"-atitude Blockbuster quiz game) 15, 20-21

CHILD OF GOD: I Am a Child of God (paper dolls) 23, 25-26

CHILD OF GOD: My Body (Image of God look-alike two-sided puzzle)   23, 27

CHILD OF GOD: My Heavenly Home (Premortal Life/Earth Life quiz) . . 23, 28

FAITH: My Faith in Jesus Grows (plant seeds in a labeled cup) 30, 33

FAITH is Cool! (Made in the shade with Heavenly Father's Plan glasses) 30, 34-35

FAITH: I Will Stand for Right like Alma (persecution flip story)...31, 36-37

FAITH: I Will Be Strong in Faith (Faith-ful Saints guessing game) 31, 38-39

FASTING Helps Me Grow Close to Heavenly Father (fasting tree)...41, 43-44

FASTING to Invite the Spirit (Fasting with PIZZA doorknob reminder)...41, 45

FORGIVENESS: I Am Happy when I Forgive (forgiving faces)......47, 49-50

FORGIVE: Jesus Said Forgive (Joseph and brothers finger puppets)......47, 51

FORGIVENESS: Plan for Redemption (King Lamoni's father story)......47, 52

HONESTY: I Am Happy when Honest (smile and frown hand puppet)....54, 56

HONESTY: Tell the Truth (Trevor and Trina Truth sack puppets).....54, 57-58

OBEDIENCE: Parents Help Me Learn Commandments (slide-show).....61, 64

OBEDIENCE: I Have "Bean" Obedient (jelly bean bag)...........61, 65-66

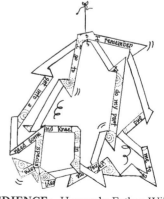

OBEDIENCE: Heavenly Father Will Help Me Obey (message dangler)..62, 67

OBEDIENCE: Obey like Alma and Amulek (missionary flip story) 62, 68-69

PRAYER: To Heavenly Father I Pray (Daniel & lions' den drama scene) 71, 74

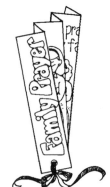

PRAYER: I Like to Pray with My Family (family prayer fan) 71, 75

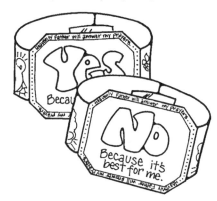

PRAYER: Heavenly Answers My Prayers ("YES," "NO" wristbands) 71, 76

PRAYER: I Pray to Heavenly Father (Monday - Sunday prayer elevator) 72, 77

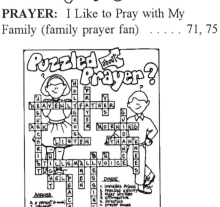

PRAYER: I Will Seek Heavenly Father's Guidance (prayer crossword puzzle) 72, 78

PRAYER Decisions (Then and Now Challenge obstacle course game) 72, 79-82

PRIESTHOOD Blessings: Priesthood Heals (band-aid bandelo) 84, 87

PRIESTHOOD Blessings and Ordinances (spiral kite to fly in the wind) . . . 84, 88

PRIESTHOOD Can Help Me ("Peace, be still" moving ship scene) 84, 89-90

PRIESTHOOD Power (plug into Priesthood Power lines) 85, 91

PRIESTHOOD Keys Unlock Heavenly Powers (doorknob reminder) 85, 92

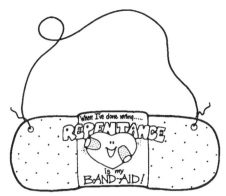
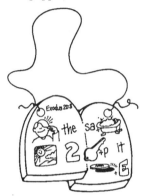

PRIESTHOOD: Heavenly Keys (priesthood keys crossword puzzle) 85, 93

REPENTANCE Heals (repentance bandage breastplate) 95, 98

REPENTANCE: I Can Say I'm Sorry (hippo sack puppet) 95, 99

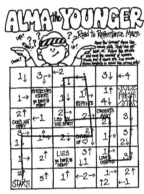

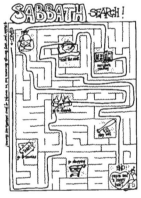

REPENTANCE (Alma the Younger's Road to Repentance maze) 96, 100

REPENTANCE: Jesus Made it Possible (Repentance puzzle) 96, 101

SABBATH DAY: A Day to Remember (Sabbath Day medallion) 103, 106

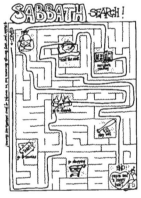

SABBATH DAY: I Want to Worship at Church (Sunday block game) . . 103, 107

SABBATH: Keep the Sabbath Day Holy (Decision Drama or Draw) 104, 108-109

SABBATH DAY: Choose Activities ("Sabbath Search" maze) 104, 110

SACRAMENT: Remembering Jesus (Last Supper shadow box) 112, 115

SACRAMENT: Promises (sacrament and baptism covenant flip-card) 112, 116

SACRAMENT: I Remember Jesus (sacrament manners match game) 113, 117

SACRAMENT: I Will Remember Jesus (sacrament symbols puzzle) . . . 113, 118

TESTIMONY (bear slide show doorknob hanger) 120, 123-124

TESTIMONY: I Can "Bear" My Testimony (find secret message) 120, 125

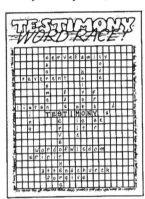

TESTIMONY: Things that Strengthen (TESTIMONY word race) 121, 126

TESTIMONY (What Would Jesus Do? choice situation sack) 121, 127

TITHING: I Can Pay Tithing (tithing purse with coins) . . 129, 132-133

TITHING: I Can Show Love As I Share (tithing envelope) 129, 134

TITHING: I Will Pay a Full Tithing (origami tithing purse/wallet) . . 130, 135

TITHING: I Want to Pay My Tithing (tithing bills match game) 130, 136

WORD OF WISDOM: I Am Thankful for Food (food and cupboard) . 138, 140

WORD OF WISDOM: I Eat Healthy (Word of Wisdom choices) 138, 141-142

WORD OF WISDOM: I Will Say "No" to Harmful Things (voting ballot) 138, 143

ARTICLES OF FAITH: *I Believe in the Church of Jesus Christ*

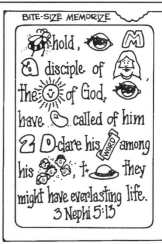

BITE-SIZE MEMORIZE

Behold, M a disciple of the [Son] of God, have [been] called of him 2 [to] declare his [word] among his [people], t[hat] they might have everlasting life. 3 Nephi 5:13

PREPARE AHEAD: Scripture Lesson, Bite-size Memorize Poster, Activity, and Thought Treat

OPENING SONG/PRAYER: "The Fourth Article of Faith," page 124 in the Children's Songbook*

BITE-SIZE MEMORIZE: Present the 3 Nephi 5:13 poster (shown right) on page 3. Color poster and display to learn.

SCRIPTURE LESSON: Search and ponder scriptures below.

> **ARTICLES OF FAITH:**
> *I Believe in the Church of Jesus Christ*

Articles of Faith #1-13—*Pearl of Great Price** written by the prophet Joseph Smith, telling our beliefs. See *Doctrine and Covenants Stories** (how Articles of Faith came about—pages 149-150).

\#   Key Words:

1   GODHEAD . . . . D&C 76:11-14, 20; 130:22, Matthew 3:16-17, Joseph Smith—History 1:17,
. . . . *Book of Mormon Reader** "How We Got the Book of Mormon," pages 6-8

2   ADAM . . . . Ezekiel 18:20, Revelation 20:12, 2 Corinthians 5:10,
. . . . *Old Testament Stories** "Adam and Eve," pages 15-18

3   ATONEMENT . . . . Hebrews 5:9, D&C 93:38, Helaman 5:9
. . . . *New Testament Stories** "Jesus Suffers in the Garden of Gethsemane," page 111-114

4   PRINCIPLES . . . . *Faith:* Hebrews 12:2, Galatians 3:26, *Repentance:* Proverbs 28:13,
. . . . *Baptism:* D&C 20:72-74, John 3:5, *Holy Ghost:* D&C 35:6

5   CALLED . . . . D&C 20:60; 42:11, John 15:16

6   PRIMITIVE . . . . Ephesians 4:11-12, *D&C Stories** "Priesthood Leaders," pages 140-144

7   GIFT . . . . 1 Corinthians 12:7-10

8   BIBLE . . . . 1 Nephi 13:24-26, D&C 26:1; 35:20; 42:12, Primary 5 manual* lesson #20,
. . . . Pearl of Great Price Introductory Note

9   REVEALED . . . . D&C 121:26-27, Amos 3:7

10 GATHERING . . . . 1 Nephi 19:16, Ether 13:6, Jeremiah 23:8, Micah 4:6-7,
*D&C Stories** page 63 (build a city named Zion where Jesus would come to live—D&C 45:64-71)

11 WORSHIP . . . . D&C 134:4

12 LAW . . . . D&C 58:21; 134:1, 6

13 HONEST . . . . Philippians 4:8, 1 Corinthians 13:4, 7

HOME-SPUN FUN ACTIVITIES: Select activities from the following pages to make learning fun.

CLOSING SONG/PRAYER: "The Thirteenth Article of Faith," page 132 in Children's Songbook*

THOUGHT TREAT: 13 Miniature Doughnuts and/or Doughnut Holes. Name the 13 gospel beliefs (the Articles of Faith). Make a copy of the 13 number/word squares (page 4). Cut out squares, tape them to toothpicks, and place in doughnuts. Talk about the doughnut hole that is missing from each doughnut and the beliefs that would be missing if we did not have the complete, restored gospel.

MORE LESSON IDEAS: IDEA #1—*Gospel Principles** "The Articles of Faith," pages 306-307
IDEA #2—Primary lessons found in the *Primary** manuals (see LESSON IDEAS on page 2)
IDEA #3—*Uniform System for Teaching the Gospel** missionary discussions #2 (2-12 - 2-19)

ARTICLES OF FAITH *Activities and Lesson Ideas*

ARTICLES OF FAITH Strengthen My Testimony
(Articles of Faith Lucky Number Game)

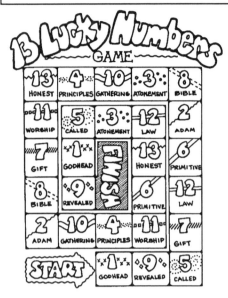

YOU'LL NEED: Copy of Articles of Faith Lucky Numbers Game board (page 4) on colored cardstock paper, two different coins (markers), and a die. Instead of using a die, write the numbers 1-5 on separate strips of paper to draw from to determine moves (make several sets of numbers 1-5).

AGES 8-TEENS: Play the Articles of Faith Lucky Numbers Game to learn the key words and learn the Articles of Faith. Color game board.
TO PLAY Articles of Faith Lucky Number Game:
1. Divide into two teams.
2. Place a marker for each team at START.
3. The first team rolls the die or chooses a 1-5 slip of paper and moves the number.
4. When team lands on a number, look at the Articles of Faith key word.

5. If person playing can say the Article of Faith, he earns 20 points for their team.
6. How to Win? Be the first team to get to FINISH, or be the first team to earn 100 points by saying their Articles of Faith.

THOUGHT TREAT: Lucky 13 Cookies. Write numbers 1, 2, 3, 4, 5, 6, 7, 8, 9, 10, 11, 12, and 13 on 13 different sugar cookies using frosting in a tube. Have the child who eats the numbered cookie recite the Article of Faith belonging to that number.

AWARD CHILDREN with an Articles of Faith card and/or large poster (available at LDS bookstores or the Church Distribution Center*).

MORE ARTICLES OF FAITH LEARNING GAMES

To play Game #1 and #2 below, copy two Articles of Faith Lucky Numbers Game boards (page 4) and cut up number/word squares to make two sets. Choose from the following activities to help children learn numbers (ages 3-5) and the key words (ages 6-Teens).

GAME #1 Lucky 13 Number Match Game. (1) Turn numbers face down and divide family into two teams. (2) Take turns turning numbers over to make a match. Older team members can help younger children make their match. After all matches are made, the team with the most matches wins!

GAME #2 Articles of Faith Key Word Toss and Tell. (1) With family in a circle and number/word squares in a bowl in the center, have one person toss the squares into the air. (2) The family members (divided into teams) rush to grab the squares. (3) Team members get together to determine how many matches they have. (4) Then they ask the other team for their number/word squares by saying the Article of Faith that matches the square they need. If they say it correctly with the help of their team, they can take the square. Keep playing until all squares are matched. If both teams cannot say the Article of Faith, look it up and read it aloud. The unknown squares must be placed in a pile in the center. Team with the most matches win.

          *Primary manuals are published by The Church of Jesus Christ of Latter-day Saints, Salt Lake City, Utah.

Be-hold, I [M]

[a] disciple of [Jesus],

the sun of God,

have been called of him

2 Declare his WORD among

his children, † that they

might have everlasting life.

3 Nephi 5:13

BAPTISM: *I Promise to Follow Jesus*

PREPARE AHEAD: Scripture Lesson, Bite-size Memorize Poster, Activity, and Thought Treat

OPENING SONG/PRAYER: "Baptism," page 100, Children's Songbook*

BITE-SIZE MEMORIZE: Present the John 3:5 poster (shown right) on page 8. Color poster and display to learn.

SCRIPTURE LESSON: Search and ponder scriptures below.

BAPTISM: *I Promise to Follow Jesus . . . Acts 2:38*

We are asked by Heavenly Father to follow Jesus and be baptized by immersion for the remission of sins, and then to receive the Holy Ghost to guide us throughout our lives.

♥ BAPTISM means we promise to follow Jesus. . . . . Matthew 3:13-17
God commands all men to repent and be baptized in his name, to receive the Holy Ghost and to follow Jesus Christ. . . . . .2 Nephi 31: 11-13, 2 Nephi 9:23, D&C 76:51-52

♥ BAPTISM means we take upon us the name of Jesus Christ . . . . Mosiah 3:17

♥ BAPTISM is a covenant or promise to serve God. . . . . Mosiah 21:35, Mosiah 18:8-10
Your reward for being baptized and serving God is eternal life (live with Heavenly Father).
. . . . Alma 7:15-16, D&C 84:74

♥ BAPTISM covenants are remembered as you partake of the sacrament . . . . . . 3 Nephi 18:5, 11, 30
The sacrament helps us remember Jesus, keep the commandments, and promises his spirit to guide us.

♥ BAPTISM is performed by the Aaronic Priesthood. . . . . D&C 13:1, D&C 84:26-27, JS-H 1:69

♥ BAPTISM should be done by immersion to "bury" your sins. . . . . D&C 76:51, 128:12

♥ BAPTISM is a principle of the gospel of Jesus Christ. . . . . .Fourth Article of Faith, D&C 39:6

♥ BAPTISM is necessary for the living and the dead to inherit celestial glory. . . . . .D&C 137:5-10

HOME-SPUN FUN ACTIVITIES: Select activities from the following pages to make learning fun.

CLOSING SONG/PRAYER: "When I Am Baptized," page 103 in the Children's Songbook*

THOUGHT TREATS:

#1 Baptism Blessing Biscuits. *Treat matches BLESSINGS FROM BAPTISM activity on the following page.* Wrap wordstrip patterns in foil and place in the center of biscuit dough or muffin batter before baking--one message for each child. As children eat, tell them to look for the message. Read message aloud. Messages match words on poster.

#2 Moo-ve Toward Baptism Milk Duds®. *Treat matches EIGHT IS GREAT activity on the following page.* Give children 8 Milk Duds® candies, a sugar cookie in the shape of an 8, or 8 candies that look like a cow's hide (black and white taffy or brown and white caramels). Children can share 8 ways they can be "udderly" responsible like Annabelle Accountable cow as they moo-ve toward baptism.

MORE LESSON IDEAS: IDEA #1—*Gospel Principles** Chapter 20 (pages 129-135)
IDEA #2—Primary lessons found in the *Primary** manuals (see LESSON IDEAS on pages 6-7)
IDEA #3—*Family Home Evening Resource Book** (pages 52-55, 120-123)
IDEA #4—*Uniform System for Teaching the Gospel** missionary discussion #2 (pages 2-16, 17)
IDEA #5—*New Testament Stories** "Jesus Is Baptized," pages 30-33 (Matthew 3:16-17, 2 Nephi 31:7-8)

*Songbook and suggested lesson materials are published by The Church of Jesus Christ of Latter-day Saints, Salt Lake City, Utah.

BAPTISM *Activities and Lesson Ideas*

I CAN BE BAPTIZED LIKE JESUS *(baptism by immersion 3-D pull-up card)*

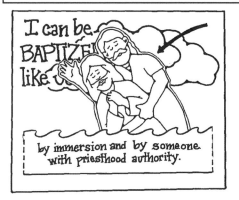

LESSON IDEAS: See lesson #11 in Primary 3-CTR B manual*.

YOU'LL NEED: Copy of baptism font and figures (page 9) on cardstock paper, and a metal or button brad for each child, scissors, glue, and crayons

AGES 3-7 ACTIVITY: Create a baptism scene to show how children can be baptized by immersion like Jesus.
A brad allows the figure to move in and out of the three-dimensional water below.
TO MAKE: (1) Color and cut out water, figures, and scene.
(2) Attach baptism figures with a metal or button brad where indicated. To Make a Button Brad: Sew two buttons together on opposite sides (threading thread through the same hole) to attach figure to paper. (3) Fan-fold water tabs and glue to scene.
(4) Move figures down to immerse in water.

BLESSINGS FROM BAPTISM INTO JESUS CHRIST'S CHURCH
(picture word poster with glue-on stickers)

LESSON IDEAS: See Lesson #21 in Primary 3-CTR B manual*.

YOU'LL NEED: Copy of poster and glue-on stickers (page 10) on colored cardstock paper for each child, scissors, glue, and crayons

AGES 3-7 ACTIVITY: Create a poster to remind children of the blessings that come from being a member of The Church of Jesus Christ of Latter-day Saints. Blessings begin with baptism.
1. Color and cut out baptism poster and glue-on stickers.
2. Read the poster together and glue on stickers.

EIGHT IS GREAT! -- Age of Accountability
(Annabelle Accountable ... the "udderly" responsible cow)

LESSON IDEAS: See lesson #27 in Primary 3-CTR B manual*.

YOU'LL NEED: Copy of cow and spots (page 11) on white cardstock paper for each child, scissors, glue, and crayons

AGES 3-7 ACTIVITY: Remind child that at age eight they can be baptized. Say, "Let's learn how to make right choices before baptism. We can be accountable, or responsible for our actions. Let's create Annabelle the accountable cow who is utterly responsible for her actions. Each spot shows ways you can be accountable." TO MAKE COW: (1) Color and cut out cow picture and spots (flaps) to cover accountable actions. (2) Fold the matching cow spot flaps. (3) Glue flaps on cow's matching spots (spot can flip open to read the accountable action).

BAPTISM *Activities and Lesson Ideas*

I PROMISE AND HEAVENLY FATHER PROMISES
(two-sided puzzle)

LESSON IDEAS: See lesson #13 in Primary 3-CTR B manual*.

YOU'LL NEED: Copy of two-sided puzzle (page 12) on colored cardstock paper, an envelope or zip-close plastic sandwich bag to store puzzle pieces for each child, glue, scissors, and crayons

AGES 7-12 ACTIVITY: Create a two-sided puzzle with child's baptism promises on one side and Heavenly Father's promises on the other side. (1) Color pictures. (2) Fold on dividing line back-to-back. (3) Glue sides together (spreading glue over the entire piece, not just the edges). (4) Trim edges. Cut puzzle shapes out as shown on one side (into six pieces). (5) Place puzzle pieces in an individual envelope or zip-close plastic sandwich bag. Give one to each child to find the puzzle message.

THOUGHT TREAT: Handprint Cookie. Place hand in rolled-out sugar cookie dough (placed on waxed paper). Remove excess dough and bake (no need to move handprint). Press jelly beans or small gumdrops in nail area before baking. Show child that we often raise our hand to promise things. Count the promises the child makes to Heavenly Father at baptism on the child's first five fingers. Then count the promises Heavenly Father makes to the child on the second hand.

I WILL KEEP MY BAPTISMAL COVENANTS
(Waters of Mormon scripture word search)

LESSON IDEAS: See lesson #12 in Primary 4 manual*

YOU'LL NEED: Copy of scripture word search (page 13) on cardstock paper for each child, scissors, glue, pencils, and crayons

AGES 8 - TEENS: Follow Alma as he leads the righteous people away from the wicked King Noah. Lead them to the Waters of Mormon where they can be baptized into Jesus Christ's church. Complete the scripture word search to get there. Then color in the Waters of Mormon. HOW TO DO WORD SEARCH: Search the scriptures to find the missing words. Then circle the missing words in the Waters of Mormon.

THOUGHT TREAT: Blueberry Punch. As children drink this blue punch, talk about the blue sky reflecting its blue color onto the Waters of Mormon as Alma baptized the saints. OPTION to Blueberry Punch (add blue food coloring to clear soda pop).

WATERS of MORMON WORD SEARCH

Search the scriptures to find the missing words then circle the word in the Word search below. Words go down, across or diagonal!

① Alma repented of his sins. (Mosiah 18:1) ② Alma did teach the people about Jesus Christ. (Mosiah 18:3) ③ Alma preached repentance, and redemption and faith on the Lord. (Mosiah 18:7) ④ Alma asked people to stand as witnesses of God. (Mosiah 18:9) ⑤ Desire in your hearts to be baptized and enter into a covenant. (Mosiah 18:10) ⑥ All this was done in the Waters of Mormon. (Mosiah 18:30) ⑦ The people who were there came to a knowledge of their Redeemer. (Mosiah 18:30) ⑧ The King sent his army to destroy them. (Mosiah 18:33) ⑨ They took their families and their tents and departed into the wilderness. (Mosiah 18:34)

Verily, verily, I say unto thee, Except a man be born of water and of the Spirit, he cannot enter into the Kingdom of God.

John 3:5

PATTERN: *BAPTISM (baptism by immersion 3-D pull-up card)*

I can be BAPTIZED like Jesus.

by immersion and by someone with priesthood authority.

BAPTISIMAL PROMISES

When I am baptized:

- ☐ ☐ come a new member of the ☐.
- ☐ will receive the ☐ of the Holy ☐.
- ☐ ☐ be ☐ given by ☐ ly Father.

PATTERN: *BAPTISM (promise two-sided puzzle)*

I PROMISE...

- to obey the commandments
- to read the scriptures
- to honor parents, help others
- to pay tithing
- to attend Primary + Sacrament meeting

Heavenly Father PROMISES...

- To forgive me when I repent
- to love and bless me
- To give me the gift of the Holy Ghost
- to answer my prayers
- to let me live with him forever

WATERS of MORMON
WORD SEARCH

Search the scriptures to find the missing words then circle the word in the word search below. Words go down, across or diagonal!

B	N	I	L	I	V	S	E	A	D	N	I	K	W	C	W
R	M	K	T	E	R	R	E	D	E	M	P	T	I	O	N
Z	O	R	B	P	B	N	T	A	N	C	E	I	I	V	O
L	R	N	A	R	M	Y	M	L	R	E	H	E	N	E	W
M	M	O	C	K	N	O	W	L	E	D	G	E	E	N	S
A	O	W	H	W	Z	F	D	E	P	S	E	V	S	A	C
R	N	H	T	T	M	L	A	T	E	N	T	S	S	N	N
S	H	E	A	R	T	S	P	I	N	O	M	Q	E	T	E
B	A	P	T	I	Z	E	D	N	T	L	O	R	S	N	T
T	F	A	M	I	L	I	E	S	E	H	M	T	H	I	S
F	T	N	U	L	C	A	N	T	D	A	W	Z	S	E	Z

① Alma _____ of his sins. (Mosiah 18:1)   ② Alma did _____ the people about Jesus Christ. (Mosiah 18:3)   ③ Alma preached _____ and _____ and _____ on the Lord. (Mosiah 18:7)
④ Alma asked people to stand as _____ of God. (Mosiah 8:9)
⑤ Desire in your _____ to be _____ and enter into a _____.
(Mosiah 18:10)   ⑥ All this was done in the Waters of _____.
(Mosiah 18:30)   ⑦ The people who were there came to a _____ of their Redeemer. (Mosiah 18:30)   ⑧ The King sent his _____ to destroy them. (Mosiah 18:33)   ⑨ They took their _____ and their _____ and departed into the wilderness. (Mosiah 18:34)

BEATITUDES: *Jesus Gave Us a Plan for Happiness*

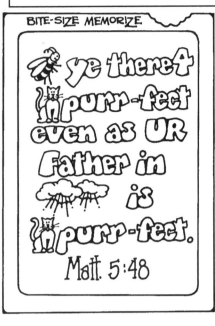

PREPARE AHEAD: Scripture Lesson, Bite-size Memorize Poster, Activity, and Thought Treat

OPENING SONG/PRAYER: "Tell Me the Stories of Jesus," page 57 in the Children's Songbook*

BITE-SIZE MEMORIZE: Present the Matthew 5:48 poster (shown right) on page 16. Color poster and display to learn.

SCRIPTURE LESSON: Search and ponder scriptures below and on the following page.

BEATITUDES: *Jesus' Plan for Happiness*

Jesus gave us the beatitudes during his Sermon on the Mount (Matthew 5:3-12) and to the Nephites in ancient America (3 Nephi 12:3-12). The beatitudes tell us a plan for happiness and ways we can get back to heaven. *"Blessed are the pure in heart: for they shall see God"* (Matthew 5:8).

As you read the beatitudes, notice how the *"poor in spirit"* beatitude is translated correctly from Matthew 5:3 to 3 Nephi 12:3: *"Blessed are the poor in spirit <u>who come unto me</u>, for theirs is the kingdom of heaven." Coming unto* Jesus Christ is learning about the teachings he gave in the scriptures. Let's start with the beatitudes.

HOME-SPUN FUN ACTIVITIES: Select activities from the following pages to make learning fun.

CLOSING SONG/PRAYER: "Choose the Right Way," page 160 in the Children's Songbook*

THOUGHT TREATS: <u>"Bee" Happy Honey Bee Taffy.</u> Serve honey taffy or honey treat and tell the children that the "bee"atitudes and other truths Jesus taught will help us "bee" happy.

MORE LESSON IDEAS: IDEA #1—Lesson ideas found in the *Primary** manuals (see page 15). IDEA #2—*New Testament Stories** "The Sermon on the Mount," pages 48-50

BEATITUDES   *Activity and Lesson Idea*

JESUS TAUGHT US HOW TO GET TO HEAVEN
("Bee"-atitude cross match)

YOU'LL NEED: Copy of "Bee"-atitude cross match (page 17) for each child, and pencils

AGES 6-TEENS ACTIVITY: Learn the beatitudes (Matthew 5:3-12) and then match the beatitude with the bee. Jesus taught the beatitudes in his Sermon on the Mount. He taught the people how to get back to heaven.
1. Color bees.
2. Draw a line from the bee to the matching beatitude.

BEATITUDES *Activities and Lesson Ideas*

JESUS TAUGHT US HOW TO BE HAPPY
("Bee"-atitude Blessing wheel)

LESSON IDEAS: See lesson #34 in Primary 4 manual* (Book of Mormon).

YOU'LL NEED: Copy of Blessing wheel (page 18) on colored cardstock paper and a metal or button brad for each child, scissors, glue, and crayons

AGES 6-11 ACTIVITY: Create a "Bee"-atitude Blessing wheel with Humble Bee, Merciful Bee, Pure in Heart Bee and more, to remind children of the truths Jesus taught the Nephites. (1) Color and cut out "Bee"-atitude Blessing wheels. (2) Attach part A on top of part B with a metal brad or button brad (placed in center).
TO MAKE BUTTON BRAD: Sew two buttons together on opposite sides (threading thread through the same holes) to attach blessing wheels.

HAVE A GOOD "BEE"-ATITUDE AND YOU'LL BUZZ THROUGH LIFE
("Bee"-atitude match puzzle)

YOU'LL NEED: Copy of dot match puzzle (page 19) on colored cardstock paper and scissors.

AGES 8-11 ACTIVITY: Cut out puzzle pieces and match up circles, dots, and hearts on all sides.

"BEE"-ATITUDE BLESSINGS
("Bee"-atitude Blockbuster quiz game)

YOU'LL NEED: Copy of quiz boxes (pages 20-21) on colored cardstock paper, scissors, crayons or markers, glue, and tape.

AGES 8 - TEENS ACTIVITY: Learn the beatitudes by guessing the missing words written on beatitude blocks.
TO MAKE BLOCKS: (1) Color and cut out blocks.
(2) Fold and glue edges, and tape down lid.
TO PLAY: Play with teams or with 2-5 players.
(1) Take turns rolling one block at a time, alternating blocks. (2) Play for Points: The first player or team who earns 100 points wins! ◘ **10 POINTS:** Land on "Bee"-atitude Blessing and find the missing word in scriptures. ◘ **20 POINTS:** Guess the missing word.
◘ **20 POINTS:** Land on "Bee"-atitude Blockbuster.
◘ **20 POINTS:** Land on Buzz Your Way to Heaven.

*Primary manual is published by The Church of Jesus Christ of Latter-day Saints, Salt Lake City, Utah.

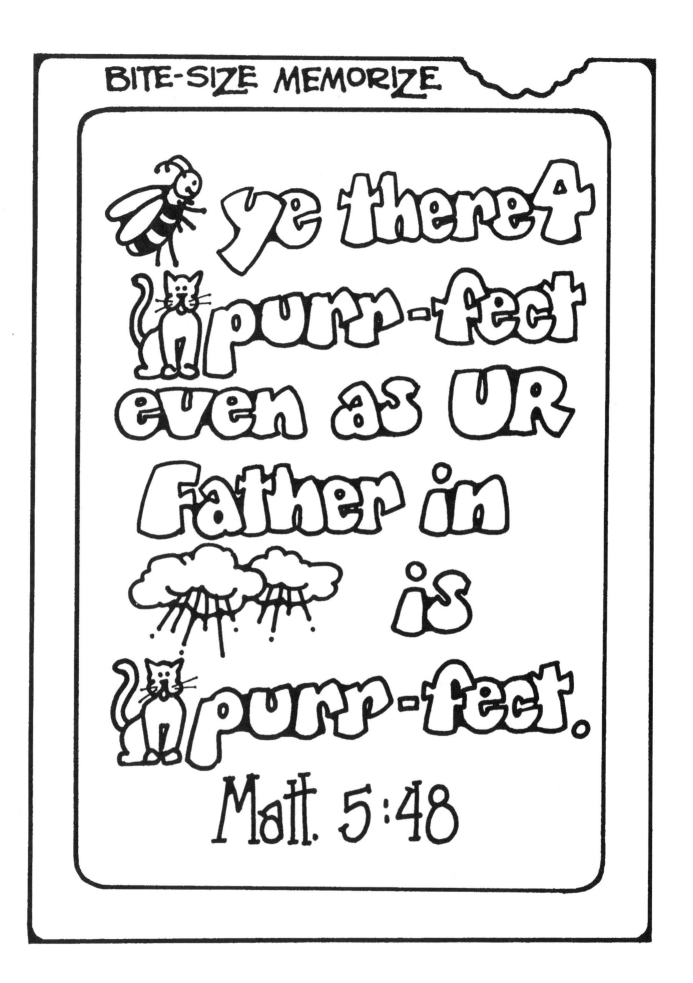

ye there 4 purr-fect even as UR Father in is purr-fect.

Matt. 5:48

BEE-ATTITUDES!

I can remember the beatitudes and buzz through life.

Matthew 5:3-12

POOR IN SPIRIT BEE

Blessed are the poor in spirit.... ○ for they shall inherit the earth.

RIGHTEOUS BEE

Blessed are they which do hunger and thirst after righteousness... ○ for they shall obtain mercy.

PURE IN HEART BEE

Blessed are the pure in heart.... ○ for theirs is the Kingdom of heaven.

MEEK BEE

Blessed are the meek.... ○ for they shall be comforted.

MERCIFUL BEE

Blessed are the merciful... ○ for they shall be filled.

MOURNING BEE

Blessed are they that mourn.... ○ for they shall be called the children of God.

PEACEMAKER BEE

Blessed are the peacemakers... ○ for they shall see God.

PATTERN: *BEATITUDES ("Bee"-atitude Blessing wheel part A)*

PATTERN: *BEATITUDES ("Bee"-atitude Blessing wheel part B)*

Persecuted for Right

Peacemaker

Poor in Spirit

Pure in Heart

Mourning

Have a good BEE-ATTITUDE buzz and you'll get through life!

Merciful

Righteous

Love

Meek

Light

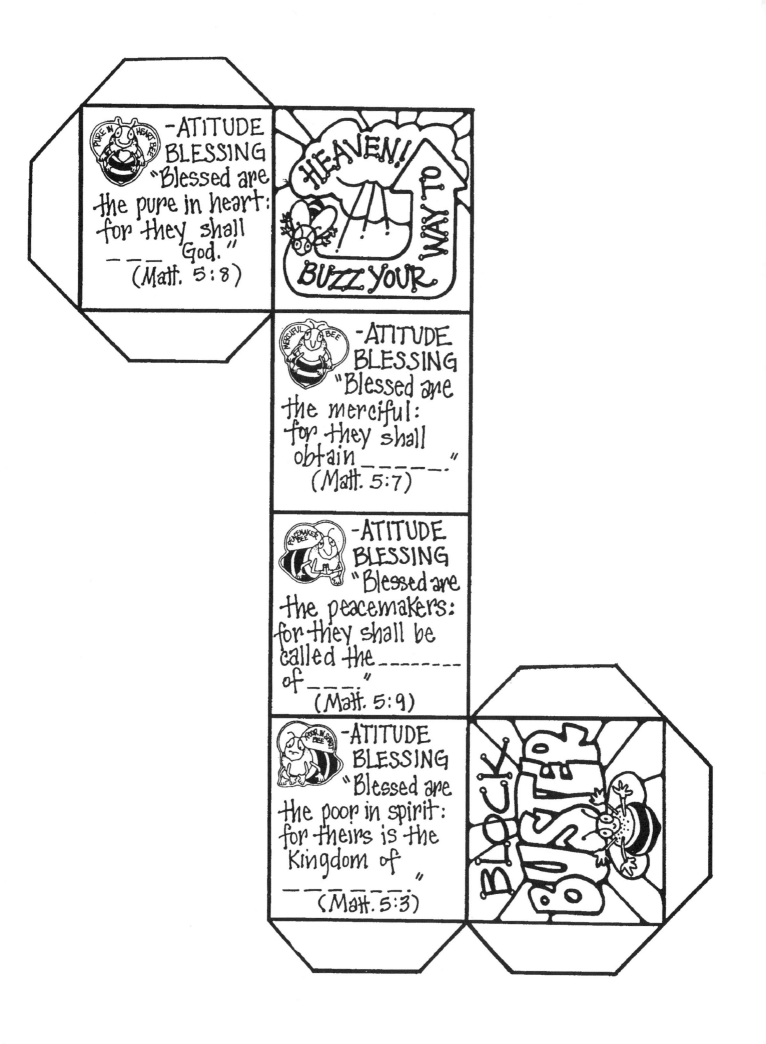

CHILD OF GOD: *My Heavenly Father Loves Me*

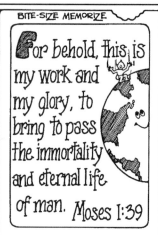

BITE-SIZE MEMORIZE

For behold, this is my work and my glory, to bring to pass the immortality and eternal life of man. Moses 1:39

PREPARE AHEAD: Scripture Lesson, Bite-size Memorize Poster, Activity, and Thought Treat

OPENING SONG/PRAYER: "I Am a Child of God," page 2 in the Children's Songbook*

BITE-SIZE MEMORIZE: Present the Moses 1:39 poster (shown right) on page 24. Color poster and display to learn.

SCRIPTURE LESSON: Search and ponder scriptures below and on the following page.

CHILD OF GOD: Heavenly Father Loves Us

♥ **GOD IS OUR HEAVENLY FATHER** . . . Alma 30:44, Psalms 82:6

God lives in heaven. . . . . .D&C 20:17

God sent his son Jesus Christ to create the heavens and the earth and us. . . . . .Moses 2:1

God sent his son Jesus Christ to die for us so that we might be forgiven of our sins, so we can live with God again. . . . . 1 Nephi 11:33, 2 Nephi 10:25, Moses 1:39 (poster above)

CHILD OF GOD VISUALS: For children ages 3-7, use paper dolls on pages 25-26 and discuss the following points (written on dolls).

♥ **I AM A CHILD OF GOD:**

I was created in the image of God (Heavenly Father and Jesus). . .Genesis 1:26-27, D&C 130:22

I am not alone. Heavenly Father will lead and guide me . . . . D&C 112:10

Heavenly Father and Jesus sent the Holy Ghost to dwell in my heart . . . . D&C 130:22

Heavenly Father answers my prayers. . . . . . ."A Child's Prayer," page 12 in Children's Songbook*

♥ **I AM HIS SPIRIT CHILD:** . . . . John 17:3

I lived in heaven. . . . . .D&C 138:55-56

I am Heavenly Father's spirit child. . . . . D&C 93:33

I will be able to recognize truth when I hear it through the Spirit. . . . . .John 18:37

Heavenly Father wants me to keep the commandments so I can live with him again. . .D&C 14:7

♥ **MY HEAVENLY FATHER LOVES ME:**

Because Heavenly Father loves me, he wants me to serve others . . . . Mosiah 4:15

HOME-SPUN FUN ACTIVITIES: Select activities from the following pages to make learning fun.

CLOSING SONG/PRAYER: "My Heavenly Father Loves Me," page 228 in Children's Songbook*

THOUGHT TREATS: <u>Boy or Girl Cookies</u>. Idea #1: Make gingerbread boys and girls. Idea #2: Make sugar cookie boys and girls (color clothes with frosting or paint cookie dough before baking). Cookie Paints: Mix two teaspoons canned milk with food coloring.

MORE LESSON IDEAS: IDEA #1—*Gospel Principles** Chapter 1 and 2

IDEA #2—Primary lessons found in the *Primary** manuals (see LESSON IDEAS on page 23)

IDEA #3—*Family Home Evening Resource Book** (pages 20-21, 116)

IDEA #4—*Uniform System for Teaching the Gospel** missionary discussions #4 (pages 4-6, 7, 8, 9)

IDEA #5—*New Testament Stories** "Jesus Blesses Children," page 91—Mark 10:14-15

IDEA #6—*New Testament Stories** "Before the New Testament," pages 7-9—Abraham 3:24-26, and
          Old Testament Stories* "Before the Old Testament," pages 6-7—Hebrews 2:14, D&C 29:36-39

IDEA #7—*Book of Mormon Reader** (Jesus prayed for and blessed each child), page 92—3 Nephi 17:21

*Songbook and suggested lesson materials are published by The Church of Jesus Christ of Latter-day Saints, Salt Lake City, Utah.

CHILD OF GOD *Activities and Lesson Ideas*

CHILD: I Am a Child of God
(paper dolls)

LESSON IDEAS: See lesson #1 in Primary 1 manual*.

YOU'LL NEED: Copy of boy or girl paper doll set (pages 25-26) on colored cardstock paper for each child, scissors, and crayons

AGES 3-7 ACTIVITY: Create paper dolls to remind each child they are a spirit child of our Heavenly Father. (1) Color and cut out a girl or boy paper doll with matching clothes. (2) Fold flaps down on clothes to hold them on the doll.

BODY: My Body Looks Like Heavenly Father and Jesus
(look-alike two-sided puzzle)

LESSON IDEAS: See lesson #2 in Primary 1 manual*.

YOU'LL NEED: Copy of two-sided puzzle (page 27) on cardstock paper, an envelope or zip-close plastic sandwich bag to store puzzle pieces for each child, scissors, glue, and crayons

AGES 3-7 ACTIVITY: Create a two-sided puzzle with Heavenly Father and Jesus on one side, and children on the other side to show that we are created in their image. (1) Color pictures. (2) Fold pictures in half on dividing line back-to-back. (3) Glue pictures together (spreading glue over the entire piece, not just the edges). (4) Trim edges. Cut puzzle shapes out as shown on one side (into six pieces). (5) Place puzzle in an envelope or plastic bag.

CHILD OF GOD: I Can Return to My Heavenly Home
(Premortal Life/Earth Life quiz)

LESSON IDEAS: See lesson #28 in Primary 5 manual*.

YOU'LL NEED: Copy of quiz (page 28) on colored cardstock paper for each child, crayons, and plastic sheet protectors (see FUN IDEA)

AGES 8-TEENS ACTIVITY: Tell children that their faith grows as they make right choices. Let's think about the choice we made to come to earth and write it in the Premortal Life circle. Then, think about the choices you make on earth to pass the test, to go back to your heavenly home. OPTION: Use as a teaching tool. Children can cut out circles and arrow and children to show the bodies moving from premortal life to earth life. FUN IDEA: Cut out a plastic doll using plastic sheet protectors and paper doll pattern (cut head on fold line). Plastic spirit should have two sides to slip over paper doll when showing how spirit enters and leaves the body.

*Primary manuals are published by the Church of Jesus Christ of Latter-day Saints, Salt Lake City, Utah.

BITE-SIZE MEMORIZE

For behold, this is my work and my glory, to bring to pass the immortality and eternal life of man. Moses 1:39

PATTERN: *Child of God paper doll*

PATTERN: *Child of God paper doll*

PATTERN: *I have a Body—look-alike two-sided puzzle*

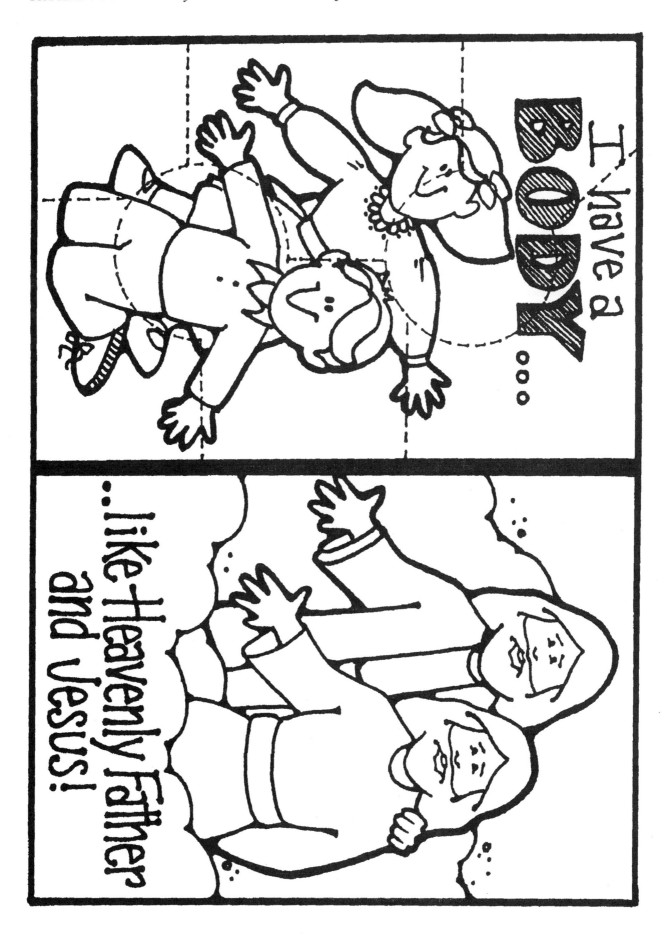

28

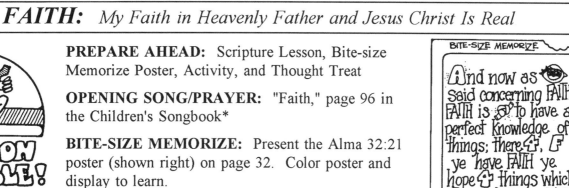

FAITH: *My Faith in Heavenly Father and Jesus Christ Is Real*

PREPARE AHEAD: Scripture Lesson, Bite-size Memorize Poster, Activity, and Thought Treat

OPENING SONG/PRAYER: "Faith," page 96 in the Children's Songbook*

BITE-SIZE MEMORIZE: Present the Alma 32:21 poster (shown right) on page 32. Color poster and display to learn.

SCRIPTURE LESSON: Search and ponder scriptures below and on the following page.

BITE-SIZE MEMORIZE

And now as said concerning FAITH- FAITH is not to have a perfect knowledge of things; there4, IF ye have FAITH ye hope 4 things which R not seen which R true.
- Alma 32:21 -

FAITH: *My Faith in Heavenly Father and Jesus Christ Is Real*

Faith that Jesus Christ and Heavenly Father love us will give us confidence to walk our path in life.

♥ FAITH is *"hope for things which are not seen, which are true."* . . . . Alma 32:21
♥ FAITH is like a seed we can plant and grow. . . . . .Alma 32:28, 42-43
♥ FAITH that Heavenly Father loved us so much that he gave us his Son Jesus to follow. . . .John 3:16
♥ FAITH that Jesus Christ will lead us to salvation. . . . . . Mosiah 3:12, Acts 4:10, 12, 2 Nephi 9:23
♥ FAITH that Joseph Smith restored the gospel of Jesus Christ to the earth in these latter days. . . . . . .
. . . . Acts 3:20-22, Amos 8:11-12, Joseph Smith History 1:17-19
♥ FAITH that the gospel of Jesus Christ is a marvelous work and a wonder. . . . . .Isaiah 29:14
♥ FAITH that the priesthood of God is restored. . . . . .Joseph Smith History 1:68-72
♥ FAITH that the Church of Jesus Christ is God's true church. . . . D&C 20 (preface—Joseph Smith testimony)
♥ FAITH that we are led by a living prophet of God today. .D&C 105:10
♥ FAITH that if we believe in the words of the prophet we shall have eternal life. . . . . . . .D&C 20:26
♥ FAITH can increase by studying the scriptures and living the gospel. . Matthew 17:20, Alma 32:27-29
♥ FAITH is increased by praying to our Heavenly Father in the name of Jesus Christ. . . Alma 34:17-25
♥ FAITH with works is alive and real, so we must <u>DO</u> all we can to increase our faith. . . . James 2:17
♥ FAITH brings miracles and blessings . . . . Moroni 7:25-26, 36-37
♥ FAITH makes it possible to be healed by priesthood power. . . . . .Alma 15:8, D&C 107:18
♥ FAITH, hope, and charity are vital so we can be pure as Jesus Christ is pure. . . . . . .Moroni 7:40-48

HOME-SPUN FUN ACTIVITIES: Select activities from the following pages to make learning fun.

CLOSING SONG/PRAYER: "I Know My Father Lives," page 5 in Children's Songbook*

THOUGHT TREAT: <u>Apple Seeds of Faith</u>. Divide an apple in half to show children the seeds that were planted in the ground to create an apple tree. Our own seeds of faith need to be planted every day if we are to keep our testimony tree growing.

MORE LESSON IDEAS: IDEA #1—*Family Home Evening Resource Book** (pages 43-47, 138-139)
IDEA #2—*Gospel Principles** Chapter 18 (pages 117-121)
IDEA #3—Primary lessons found in the *Primary** manuals (see LESSON IDEAS on pages 30-31)
IDEA #4—*Uniform System for Teaching the Gospel** missionary discussion #2 (pages 2-12, 13)
IDEA #5—*Book of Mormon Reader** "The Brother of Jared and the Jaredites," page 13 (Ether 3:7-9)
IDEA #6—*The New Testament Stories** "The Ten Lepers," pages 86-87 (Luke 17:12-19)

*Songbook and suggested lesson materials are published by The Church of Jesus Christ of Latter-day Saints, Salt Lake City, Utah.

FAITH Activities and Lesson Ideas

FAITH: I Can Plant and Grow Seeds of Faith
("My Faith in Jesus Grows" seeds planted in a plastic cup)

LESSON IDEAS: See lesson #29 in Primary 3-CTR B manual*.

YOU'LL NEED: Copy of label for planter cup (page 33) on colored cardstock paper, and two 8-ounce plastic cups, potting soil, and seeds for each child, scissors, glue or tape, and crayons

AGES 3-7 ACTIVITY: Create a pot to plant seeds in for each child to remind them that their faith in Jesus can grow. It starts as a small seed and grows into a testimony as they choose the right.
1. Color and cut out pot label.
2. Make a pot by placing two 8-ounce plastic cups inside each other (for durability). Punch a small hole in the bottom for drainage.
3. Glue or tape label on cup.
4. Fill cup half way with potting soil, drop in seeds, and fill the other half with potting soil. Have children water plant when they get home.

FAITH: My Testimony Grows As I Have Faith
(Faith Is Cool! sun glasses with watermelon glass case)

YOU'LL NEED: Copy of Faith Is Cool! sun glasses and watermelon glass case (pages 34-35) on colored cardstock paper for each child, scissors, glue, crayons, and razor blade.

AGES 3-Teens ACTIVITY: Create glasses and glass case to remind children that their testimony grows as they have faith in the Lord Jesus Christ (Mark 11:24). Place glasses in watermelon glass case for safekeeping. Tell children, "Faith is Cool! We have it made in the shade with Heavenly Father's plan."
TO MAKE GLASSES: (1) Color and cut out glasses. Parents, use a razor blade to "cut out" glasses center pieces. (2) Glue or tape side frames on glasses to fit child.
TO MAKE GLASS CASE: (1) Color and cut out watermelon pocket. (2) Glue around inside edge 1/4 inch, leaving top open to insert glasses.

THOUGHT TREAT: <u>Watermelon Cookies</u>. Cut out sugar cookie dough into 4- or 5-inch round shapes and cut in half. Bake, cool, and frost with red frosting and then edge cookie with green for the rind. Top with miniature chocolate chips. As you eat cookies, read Matthew 17:20 and say: "The scriptures will help me increase my faith in Jesus."

FAITH *Activities and Lesson Ideas*

FAITH: I Will Stand for Right like Alma and Amulek
(persecution flip story)

LESSON IDEAS: See lesson #16 in Primary 4 manual*.

YOU'LL NEED: Copy of flip story pictures (page 36) on cardstock paper, and flip story cue cards #1-6 (page 37) on lightweight paper, scissors, glue, tape, paper punch, string, and crayons.
OPTION: Page reinforcements (see #3 below).

ACTIVITY: Help children develop faith in Jesus Christ so they can stand for the right. Create a flip story to show how Alma and Amulek made a commitment to stand for right. See another Alma and Amulek flip story on pages 62, 68-69 (subject: Obedience).
TO MAKE FLIP STORY: (1) Color and cut out picture cards #1-6. Cut out cue cards #1-6. (2) Glue cue cards #1-6 on backs of picture cards. Be sure to start by gluing cue card #1 on the back of picture #6. Don't cut instructions off cue cards. (3) Tape over holes before punching holes, or punch holes and use page reinforcements. (4) Place string loosely through holes and tie.

THOUGHT TREAT: Sunflower Seeds. Help children "plant" these seeds in their mouth as you say: "Plant the seeds of faith every day by reading the scriptures and following Jesus."

FAITH: I Will Be Strong in Faith
(Faith-ful Saints guessing game)

LESSON IDEAS: See lesson #43 in Primary 4 manual*.

YOU'LL NEED: Copy of guessing game pictures and clue cards (pages 38-39) on colored cardstock paper, scissors, glue, and crayons

AGES 8-11 ACTIVITY: Encourage children to exercise their faith in Jesus Christ, play the Faith-ful Saints guessing game. TO MAKE GAME:
(1) Color and cut out pictures and clue cards.
(2) Lay picture cards on the floor or table face up.
(3) Lay clue cards in a pile face down.
TO PLAY: Divide into two teams and take turns drawing a clue card. Read the Faith-ful Saint description and guess which picture card it matches. If the guess is wrong, the other team has a chance to guess. When the guess is right, that team collects the matching picture and cue card. The team with the most cards wins.

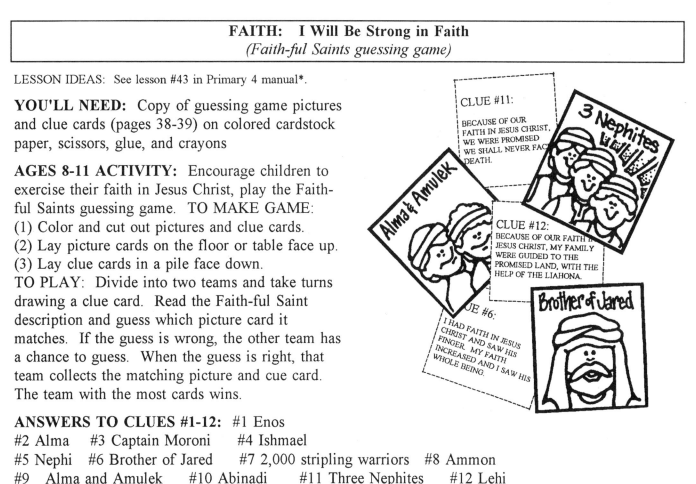

ANSWERS TO CLUES #1-12: #1 Enos
#2 Alma   #3 Captain Moroni   #4 Ishmael
#5 Nephi   #6 Brother of Jared   #7 2,000 stripling warriors   #8 Ammon
#9 Alma and Amulek   #10 Abinadi   #11 Three Nephites   #12 Lehi

BITE-SIZE MEMORIZE

And now as 👁 said concerning FAITH — FAITH is 🔦 to have a perfect knowledge of things; there 4, F ye have FAITH ye hope 4 things which R 🔦 seen which R true.

— Alma 32:21 —

PATTERN: *FAITH: ("My Faith in Jesus Grows" seeds planted in an 8-ounce plastic cup)*

Glue or tape here

My faith in
Jesus
Christ
can grow!

It will start
as a small
seed and
grow into a
testimony!

PATTERN: *FAITH (testimony glass case for watermelon Faith Is Cool! glasses)*

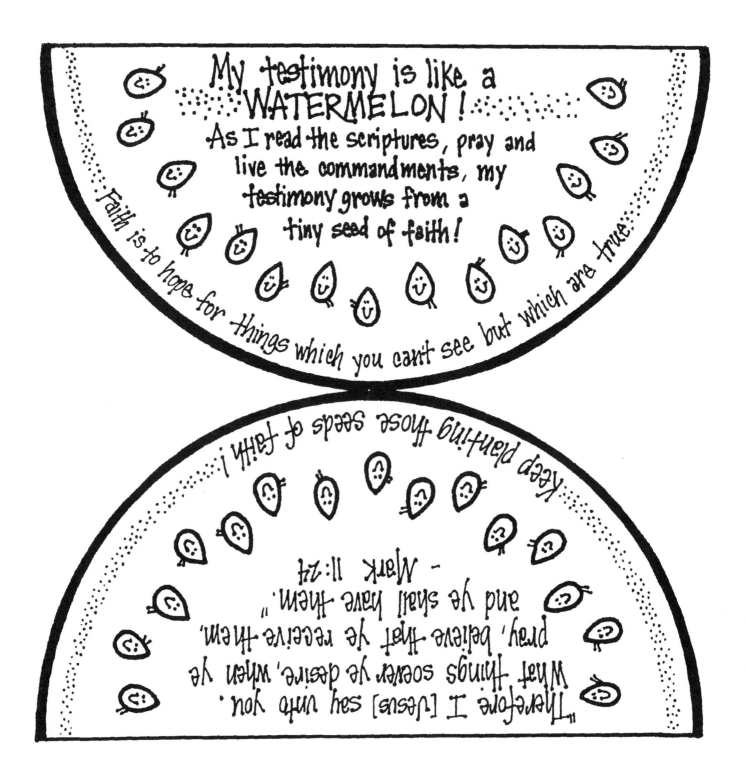

My testimony is like a
WATERMELON!
As I read the scriptures, pray and
live the commandments, my
testimony grows from a
tiny seed of faith!

Faith is to hope for things which you can't see but which are true.

Keep planting those seeds of faith!

"Therefore I [Jesus] say unto you,
What things soever ye desire, when ye
pray, believe that ye receive them,
and ye shall have them."
- Mark 11:24

PATTERN: *FAITH (persecution flip story)*

PATTERN: *FAITH (persecution flip story)*

I Will Stand for Right

God chose Alma the Younger to be the leader of the church. He loved the people and wanted them to be righteous. He felt sad when he saw that some of the people were wicked. Alma wanted to teach the people to obey God's commandments.

CUE CARD #1 - Glue to back of picture card #6

An angel told Alma the Younger to go back to the city of Ammonihah to tell the people to repent or they would be destroyed. In that city, Zeezrom was trying to blind the minds of the people with wickedness. Zeezrom listened, repented, and asked Alma the Younger and Amulek to teach him.

CUE CARD #2 - Glue to back of picture card #1

The wicked people in Ammonihah threw the righteous women and children into a pit of fire because they believed in Jesus Christ. The Holy Ghost told Alma the Younger to stand back, that the Lord would receive them into heaven. The people who were thrown into the fire would enter into the kingdom of God.

CUE CARD #3 - Glue to back of picture card #2

Alma the Younger and Amulek were thrown into prison. They were not given food and water, and they were beaten. They prayed and God helped them break the ropes. The earth shook and the prison walls fell. They walked out of prison, and the people of Ammonihah were afraid of them.

CUE CARD #4 - Glue to back of picture card #3

Alma the Younger and Amulek left Ammonihah to go to the city of Sidom. Many people in this city believed them. Zeezrom was there and felt sorry for the wicked things he had done. Alma the Younger and Amulek found him sick and blessed him. Zeezrom was healed and was baptized by Alma the Younger.

CUE CARD #5 - Glue to back of picture card #4

Zeezrom went to teach the people the gospel of Jesus Christ. Alma the Younger and Amulek baptized many and chose many leaders and teachers for Christ's church. I, too, will stand for the right and follow Jesus like Alma the Younger and Amulek.

CUE CARD #6 - Glue to back of picture card #5

PATTERN: *FAITH (Faith-ful Saints guessing game pictures #1-12)*

PATTERN: *FAITH (Faithful Saints Guessing Game clues #1-12)*

CLUE #1: I USED MY FAITH IN JESUS CHRIST AS I PRAYED DAY AND NIGHT.	**CLUE #2:** BECAUSE OF MY FAITH AND PRAYERS, AN ANGEL APPEARED TO MY SON AND FOUR SONS OF MOSIAH, CALLING THEM TO REPENTANCE.	**CLUE #3:** I USED THE TITLE OF LIBERTY FLAG TO ENCOURAGE MY PEOPLE TO HAVE FAITH IN JESUS CHRIST AND FIGHT FOR LIBERTY.
CLUE #4: I CHOSE TO TAKE MY FAMILY AND GO WITH LEHI INTO THE WILDERNESS. THIS I DID BECAUSE OF MY FAITH.	**CLUE #5:** I HAD FAITH THAT I COULD RETURN TO JERUSALEM TO GET THE BRASS PLATES. THESE WERE SACRED RECORDS KEPT BY THE PROPHETS.	**CLUE #6:** I HAD FAITH IN JESUS CHRIST AND SAW HIS FINGER. MY FAITH INCREASED AND I SAW HIS WHOLE BEING.
CLUE #7 OUR MOTHERS TAUGHT US TO HAVE FAITH. OUR FAITH TAUGHT BY OUR MOTHERS SAVED US IN BATTLE.	**CLUE #8** I DESIRED TO PREACH THE GOSPEL. MY FAITH HELPED ME FIGHT OFF A BAND OF ROBBERS TRYING TO KILL KING LAMONI'S SHEEP.	**CLUE #9:** WHILE TRYING TO PREACH REPENTANCE IN THE CITY, WE WERE CAST INTO PRISON. OUR FAITH CAUSED THE PRISON WALLS TO TUMBLE.
CLUE #10: BECAUSE OF MY FAITH IN JESUS CHRIST, I WAS WILLING TO DIE FOR MY TESTIMONY (AT THE HANDS OF KING NOAH).	**CLUE #11:** BECAUSE OF OUR FAITH IN JESUS CHRIST, WE WERE PROMISED WE SHALL NEVER FACE DEATH.	**CLUE #12:** BECAUSE OF OUR FAITH IN JESUS CHRIST, MY FAMILY WAS GUIDED TO THE PROMISED LAND, WITH THE HELP OF THE LIAHONA.

ANSWERS found on page 31 or in the following scriptures:

Clue #1 Enos 1:3-4   Clue #2 Alma 36:6-10   Clue #3 Alma 46:12-13   Clue #4 I Nephi 7:2, 4-5

Clue #5 I Nephi 4:1-31   Clue #6 Ether 3, 12:30   Clue #7 Alma 56:44-56   Clue #8 Alma 17:29-18:3, 26:12

Clue #9 Alma 14:26-28   Clue #10 Mosiah 17:7-20   Clue #11 3 Nephi 28:1-7   Clue #12 1 Nephi 16:28-29; 18:23

FASTING: *My Spirit Grows As I Fast*

PREPARE AHEAD: Scripture Lesson, Bite-size Memorize Poster, Activity, and Thought Treat

OPENING SONG/PRAYER: "Dare to Do Right," page 158 in the Children's Songbook*

BITE-SIZE MEMORIZE: Present the 3 Nephi 13:16-18 poster (shown right) on page 42. Color poster and display to learn.

SCRIPTURE LESSON: Search and ponder scriptures below and on the following page.

BITE-SIZE MEMORIZE

3 Nephi 13:16-18

Moreover, when ye fast be not as the hypocrites, of a sad countenance, for they disfigure their faces that they may appear unto men to fast. Verily I say unto you, they have their reward.
But thou, when thou fastest, anoint thy head and wash thy face;
That thou appear not unto men to fast, but unto thy Father, who is in secret; and thy Father who seeth in secret, shall reward thee openly.

FASTING: *My Spirit Grows as I Fast*

Fasting is going without food and drink for a righteous purpose.

♥ FASTING is usually done on fast Sunday, the first Sunday of the month. Fast two meals and gather for a testimony meeting. . . . . .Alma 6:6
♥ FASTING should be done by everyone who can fast. . . . . D&C 59:13-15
♥ FASTING helps us feel closer to Heavenly Father and Jesus. Alma 17:3, 9
♥ FASTING shows Heavenly Father and Jesus that we have faith. . . . D&C 88:119, Matthew 6:30-34
♥ FASTING helps us pray for special blessings. . . . . .D&C 88:76
♥ FASTING and prayer helps us know that things are true by the spirit of revelation. . . . . . .Alma 5:46
♥ FASTING should be followed by paying of fast offerings to help the poor and needy. . . . .
. . . .   D&C 88:119-120, Mosiah 4:19-21, Matthew 25:35-40, James 1:27, Jacob 2:17-19
♥ FASTING is often done with others for a cause where many fast for a purpose. . . . 3 Nephi 27:1-2,
. . . . Mosiah 27:22-23,
♥ FASTING should be done with a smile, cheerfully. . . . . .2 Corinthians 9:7, D&C 59:15
♥ FASTING brings you joy. . . . . .D&C 59:13
♥ FASTING should be done in secret. . . . . Matthew 6:1-4; 16-18
♥ FASTING helps in missionary work. . . . . Alma 6:6

HOME-SPUN FUN ACTIVITIES: Select activities from the following pages to make learning fun.

CLOSING SONG/PRAYER: "The Lord Gave Me a Temple," page 153 in Children's Songbook*

THOUGHT TREATS: Good Samaritan Cereal. Give each person a small bag of dry cereal to share with someone to show how they go without food to feed the poor and needy. Tell the story of the Good Samaritan (Luke 10:30-34). Allow everyone to receive a Good Samaritan cereal bag.

MORE LESSON IDEAS: IDEA #1—*Family Home Evening Resource Book** (pages 30, 184-185)
IDEA #2—*Gospel Principles** Chapter 25 (pages 165-169)
IDEA #3—Primary lessons found in the *Primary** manuals (see LESSON IDEAS on page 41)
IDEA #4—*Uniform System for Teaching the Gospel** missionary discussion #5 (pages 5-10, 11, 12)
IDEA #5—*Old Testament Stories** "Esther," pgs. 161-164 (asked Israelites to fast)—Esther 4:15-17
IDEA #6—*New Testament Stories** "Jesus Is Tempted," pages 34-35 (fasted 40 days)—Matthew 4:1-4

FASTING *Activities and Lesson Ideas*

FASTING: I Can Grow Closer to Heavenly Father and Jesus
(fasting tree with fruit glue-on stickers)

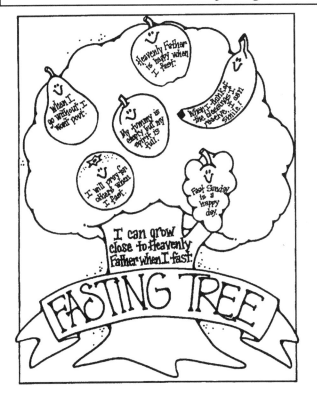

LESSON IDEAS: See lesson #41 in Primary 3-CTR B manual*.

YOU'LL NEED: Copy fasting tree (pages 43-44) on colored cardstock paper for each child, scissors, glue, and crayons

AGES 3-7 ACTIVITY: Create a fasting tree and glue six fruit smiles to show that children can grow closer to Heavenly Father as they fast.
FRUIT SMILES READ: "Fast Sunday can be a happy day. When I go without, I won't pout. When I think of the blessings I receive, I smile. I will pray for others when I fast. Heavenly Father is pleased when I fast. My tummy is empty, but my spirit is full." (1) Color and cut out fasting tree and glue-on stickers. (2) Glue stickers on tree.
(3) Have each child read or tell about how they can make fast day a happy day.

FASTING: I Can Fast to Invite the Spirit
(Try Fasting with PIZZA! doorknob fasting reminder)

YOU'LL NEED: Copy PIZZA doorknob reminder (page 45) for each child on colored cardstock paper, scissors, crayons

AGES 8-TEENS ACTIVITY: Create a PIZZA doorknob reminder children can place on their door on fast Sunday to help challenge them to fast with PIZZA: Pay fast offering. Invite the Spirit with prayer. Zip on past the kitchen! Zap hunger by reading scriptures. Ask Heavenly Father for strength.

THOUGHT TREAT: Pizza.

3 Nephi 13:16-18

Moreover, when ye fast be not as the hypocrites, of a sad countenance, for they disfigure their faces that they may appear unto men to fast. Verily I say unto you, they have their reward.

But thou, when thou fastest, anoint thy head, and wash thy face;

That thou appear not unto men to fast, but unto thy Father, who is in secret; and thy Father, who seeth in secret, shall reward thee openly.

PATTERN: *FASTING (fasting tree with fruit glue-on stickers)*

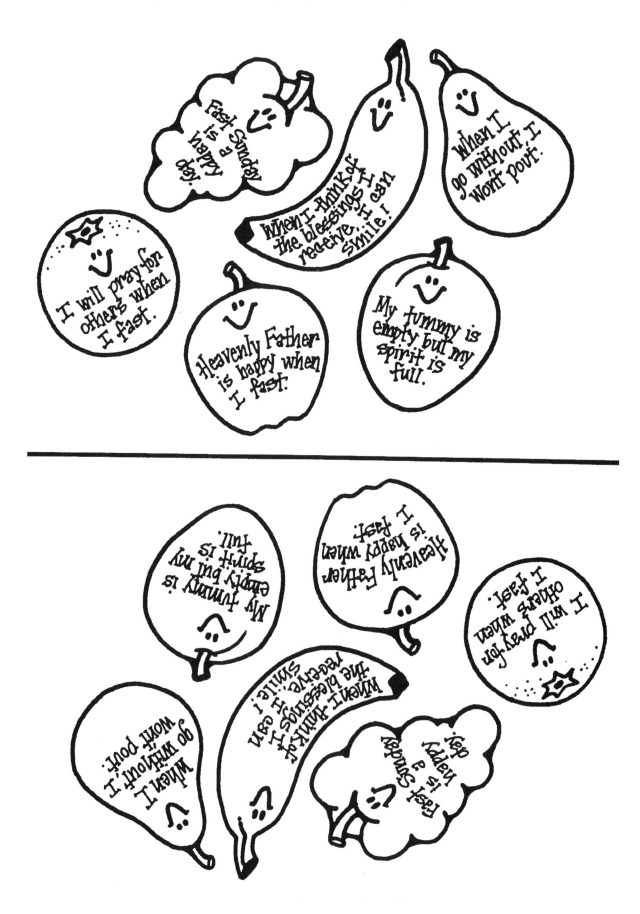

FORGIVENESS: *Jesus Wants Us to Forgive Everyone*

PREPARE AHEAD: Scripture Lesson, Bite-size Memorize Poster, Activity, and Thought Treat

OPENING SONG/PRAYER: "Jesus Said Love Everyone," page 61 in the Children's Songbook*

BITE-SIZE MEMORIZE: Present the D&C 64:10 poster (shown right) on page 48. Color poster and display to learn.

SCRIPTURE LESSON: Search and ponder scriptures below and on the following page.

BITE SIZE MEMORIZE

...the Lord. 4-give whom 4-give, but of U it is re___d to 4-give all. D&C 64:10

FORGIVENESS: Jesus Wants Us to Forgive Everyone

Tell the parable Jesus told of the prodigal son—a father forgiving his lost son. . . . . Luke 15:11-32

♥ FORGIVE others for the wrong they do and you will create peace. . . Isaiah 54:13, Matthew 18:21-22
♥ FORGIVE and love your neighbor. . . . . Matthew 5:43-46; 22:37-39, John 13:34-35
♥ FORGIVE and love your enemies. . . . . Matthew 5:44
♥ FORGIVE and be kind to everyone as God has forgiven you. . . . . Ephesians 4:32
♥ "FORGIVE all men," Jesus said. . . . . D&C 64:8-10
♥ FORGIVE others and you can be forgiven. . . . . Matthew 6:12, 14-15, 3 Nephi 13:14-15, Mark 11:25
♥ FORGIVE others like Jesus, who forgave those who crucified him. . . . . Luke 23:34
♥ FORGIVE and forget the sins of others, and Jesus forgives. . . . . D&C 58:42-43, Hebrews 8:12
♥ FORGIVE, knowing that the atonement of Jesus made it possible for all to be forgiven. . .Alma 22:14

Tell the parable Jesus told of the unmerciful servant—two men who owed money. . . . Matthew 18:23-35

HOME-SPUN FUN ACTIVITIES: Select activities from the following pages to make learning fun.

CLOSING SONG/PRAYER: "Help Me Dear Father," page 99 in the Children's Songbook*

THOUGHT TREAT: <u>Disappearing Candy</u>. Give each child a buttermint or piece of hardtack candy. Tell children, "<u>As you forgive</u> someone who has hurt you, or someone who has made you angry, those <u>ugly feelings will disappear</u> just as the hard candy disappears."

MORE LESSON IDEAS: IDEA #1—*Family Home Evening Resource Book** (pages 42, 186-187)
IDEA #2—*Gospel Principles** Chapter 19 (page 125)
IDEA #3—Primary lessons found in the *Primary** manuals (see LESSON IDEAS on page 47)
IDEA #4—*Uniform System for Teaching the Gospel** missionary discussion #2 (pages 2-14—repentance)
IDEA #5—*Old Testament Stories** "Joseph," pages 50-53 (Genesis chapter 37), "Joseph in Egypt," pages 54-57 (Genesis chapters 37-41), and "Joseph's Brothers in Egypt," pages 58-60 (Genesis chapters 41-47)

For Puppet Activity (page 47), use the following story. **JOSEPH FORGIVES HIS BROTHERS:** *Genesis 37:12-28 (Joseph's brothers sold him as a slave into Egypt), Genesis 41:38-43 (Joseph became an important man in Egypt), Genesis 42:1-8; 45:1-15 (Years later Joseph's brothers came to Egypt to get food for their country where there was a famine. They found Joseph was still alive and an important man in Egypt. Joseph felt happy to be with his brothers again. He was not angry with them. Joseph forgave and fed them).*

FORGIVENESS *Activities and Lesson Ideas*

FORGIVENESS: I Am Happy when I Forgive
(forgiving faces)

LESSON IDEAS: See lesson #40 in Primary 2-CTR A manual*.

YOU'LL NEED: Copy of situation doors and forgiving faces
(pages 49-50) on colored paper, scissors, glue, and crayons
AGES 3-7 ACTIVITY: Enjoy opening the situation doors to discover
forgiving faces. Help children understand they can be happy when they
forgive. (1) Color and cut out situation doors and forgiving faces
picture posters. (2) Glue situation doors over forgiving faces #1-4.
(3) Help children open doors to look and talk about the situations and
forgiving face responses.
THOUGHT TREAT: Funny Face
Cookies. Decorate cookies with funny
faces. Tell children that a face can tell us
many things. It can tell how a person is
feeling and forgiving.

FORGIVE: Jesus Wants Us to Forgive Everyone
(Joseph and brothers finger puppets)

LESSON IDEAS: See lesson #30 in Primary 1 manual*.

YOU'LL NEED: Copy of Joseph and brothers finger puppets (page 51)
on colored paper for each child, scissors, glue or tape, and crayons
AGES 6-11 ACTIVITY: Create Joseph and his brothers finger puppets
to act out the story of Joseph, who was sold into Egypt but forgave his
brothers. (1) Color puppets. (2) Roll puppets around a pencil to curl into
shape. (3) Cut out individual puppets and tape the back. (4) Slip puppets
over child's fingers. (5) Tell story using ideas (page 46).

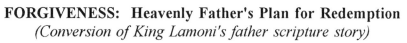

THOUGHT TREAT:
Crackers or bread made
from grain like the
grain Joseph gave his
brothers.

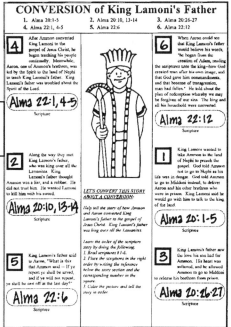

FORGIVENESS: Heavenly Father's Plan for Redemption
(Conversion of King Lamoni's father scripture story)

LESSON IDEAS: See lesson #18 in Primary 4 manual*.

YOU'LL NEED: Copy of silent story (page 52) for each
child, scissors, pencils, glue, and crayons
AGES 8-TEENS ACTIVITY: Encourage children to
find out how Ammon converted King Lamoni's father,
who learned about the plan of redemption whereby we
may be forgiven of our sins. (1) Read scriptures #1-6 at
the top. (2) Place the numbers 1-6 in right order in the
boxes below to create a scripture story. (3) Color the
pictures and read the story in order of #1-6.

👁, the Lord. 4-give whom 👁 4-give, but of ∪ it is re—d to 4-give all.

D&C 64:10

PATTERN: *FORGIVENESS (Forgiving Faces doors)*

PATTERN: *FORGIVENESS (Joseph and brothers finger puppets) . . See story ideas (page 46)*

CONVERSION of King Lamoni's Father

1. Alma 20:1-5   **2.** Alma 20:10, 13-14   **3.** Alma 20:26-27
4. Alma 22:1, 4-5   **5.** Alma 22:6   **6.** Alma 22:12

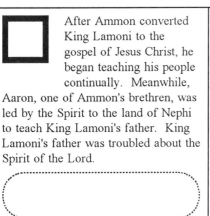 After Ammon converted King Lamoni to the gospel of Jesus Christ, he began teaching his people continually. Meanwhile, Aaron, one of Ammon's brethren, was led by the Spirit to the land of Nephi to teach King Lamoni's father. King Lamoni's father was troubled about the Spirit of the Lord.

Scripture

Along the way they met King Lamoni's father, who was king over all the Lamanites. King Lamoni's father thought Ammon was a liar, and a robber. He did not trust him. He wanted Lamoni to kill him with his sword.

Scripture

 King Lamoni's father said to Aaron, "What is this that Ammon said -- If ye repent ye shall be saved, and if ye will not repent, ye shall be cast off at the last day?"

Scripture

LET'S CONVERT THIS STORY ABOUT A CONVERSION:

Help tell the story of how Ammon and Aaron converted King Lamoni's father to the gospel of Jesus Christ. King Lamoni's father was king over all the Lamanites.

Learn the order of the scripture story by doing the following:
1. Read scriptures # 1-6.
2. Place the scriptures in the right order by writing the reference below the story section and the corresponding number in the square.
3. Color the picture and tell the story in order.

 When Aaron could see that King Lamoni's father would believe his words, "he began from the creation of Adam, reading the scriptures unto the king--how God created man after his own image, and that God gave him commandments, and that because of transgression, man had fallen." He told about the plan of redemption whereby we may be forgiven of our sins. The king and all his household were converted.

Scripture

 King Lamoni wanted to take Ammon to the land of Nephi to preach the gospel. God told Ammon not to go to Nephi as his life was in danger. God told Ammon to go to Middoni instead, to deliver Aaron and his other brethren who were in prison. King Lamoni said he would go with him to talk to the king of the land.

Scripture

 King Lamoni's father saw the love his son had for Ammon. His heart was softened, and he allowed Ammon to go to Middoni to release his brethren from prison.

Scripture

HONESTY: *I Will Tell the Truth and Be Honest*

PREPARE AHEAD: Scripture Lesson, Bite-size Memorize Poster, Activity, and Thought Treat

OPENING SONG/PRAYER: "I Believe in Being Honest," page 149, and "Dare to Do Right," page 158 in the Children's Songbook*

BITE-SIZE MEMORIZE: Present the Alma 27:27 poster (shown right) on page 55. Color poster and display to learn.

SCRIPTURE LESSON: Search and ponder scriptures below and on the following page.

BITE-SIZE MEMORIZE

And they were also distinguished for their zeal towards God, and also towards men; for they were perfectly honest and upright in all things; and they were firm in the faith of Christ, even unto the end.

Alma 27:27

> HONESTY: *I Will Tell the Truth and Be Honest*

♥ Recite the Thirteenth Article of Faith and talk about being "honest and true.". . . . . .Articles of Faith.

♥ Sing "The Thirteenth Article of Faith," page 132 in the Children's Songbook*.

♥ Story Activity: Tell the story of Barnabas, Ananias, and Sapphira. . . . . . . Acts 4:36-37; 5:1-2, 7-8. Then read the story again and have children draw Barnabus with his honest face, and Ananias and Sapphira with their dishonest faces.

♥ HONESTY is being like God who in honest and just in all things. . .D&C 3:2, Alma 7:20, Ether 3:12

♥ HONESTY is being honest in all things, firm in our faith in Jesus Christ unto the end. . Alma 27:27

♥ HONESTY is walking in the way of truth, not stealing (take others things) and not bearing false witness (lying). . . . . . . .D&C 42:21, Mosiah 4:15, Matthew 19:18, Exodus 20:15-16, Proverbs 12:22

♥ HONESTY is returning what you borrow or find (keep all pledges). . . . . D&C 136:20, 25-26

♥ HONESTY is being honest, knowing that evil actions will not save us. . . . . 2 Nephi 28:8

♥ HONESTY is working hard so we don't cheat our employer or our parents. . . . . 2 Nephi 28:8

♥ HONESTY is speaking kindly towards our neighbor. . . . . D&C 42:27; 59:6, Ephesians 4:25

♥ HONESTY is teaching others with the spirit of truth. . . . . D&C 50:17

♥ HONESTY is obeying the law of tithing and paying one tenth. . . . . .D&C 64:23; 119:4

♥ HONESTY is saying "no" to the temptation to lie. . . . . 2 Nephi 9:9

♥ DISHONEST people are deceived by Satan. . . . . D&C 10:22-28

♥ DISHONEST people will be punished. . . . . D&C 42:20-21, 84-87; 76:103-6

♥ DISHONEST people will live with Satan (the father of lies). . . . . 2 Nephi 9:9, Moses 4:4

HOME-SPUN FUN ACTIVITIES: Select activities from the following pages to make learning fun.

CLOSING SONG/PRAYER: "The Commandments," page 112, "Keep the Commandments," page 146, and "I Want to Live the Gospel," page 258 in Children's Songbook*

THOUGHT TREATS: Honest Smile and Dishonest Frown Cookies. Use frosting in a tube to decorate three cookies for each person (two with a smile and one with a frown). As you eat the smile cookie talk about honest choices that make us feel happy. As you eat the frown cookie talk about dishonest choices that make us feel sad. Finish by eating a smile cookie and talk again about honest choices that make us feel happy.

MORE LESSON IDEAS: IDEA #1—*Gospel Principles** Chapter 31 (pages 203-206) IDEA #2—Primary lessons found in the *Primary** manuals (see LESSON IDEAS on page 54) IDEA #3—*Family Home Evening Resource Book** (pages 194-196)

HONESTY *Activities and Lesson Ideas*

HONESTY: I Am Happy when I Am Honest
(smile and frown hand puppet)

LESSON IDEAS: See lesson #37 in Primary 1 manual*.

YOU'LL NEED: Copy of puppet (page 56), scissors, tape, and crayons

AGES 3-7 ACTIVITY: Create a two-sided puppet for each child to help make decisions about honesty. SMILE SIDE: Show when a choice is honest. FROWN SIDE: Show when a choice is dishonest. Read each side with children. (1) Color and cut out puppet. (2) Fold in half with smile on front and frown on back. (3) Tape outside or glue 1/4" inside on puppet top and sides, leaving the inside open for child's hand to fit in. (4) Ask children to choose which situations are honest (smile) and dishonest (frown).

HONESTY: I Will Tell the Truth *(Trevor and Trina Truth sack puppets)*

LESSON IDEAS: See lesson #34 in Primary 2-CTR A manual*.

YOU'LL NEED: Copy of girl or boy sack puppet (pages 57-58) on flesh or peach cardstock paper and a small lunch sack for each child, scissors, glue, and crayons

AGES 4-12 ACTIVITY: Sometimes it's not easy to tell the truth, but with their very own Trevor or Trina Truth sack puppets, children can role-play truth-telling situations. (1) Color and cut out Trevor for boy and Trina for girl sack puppets. (2) Glue girl or boy head to bottom of sack, and chin up under flap. When children move sack flap up and down, the puppet's mouth opens to say, "I can be strong and tell the truth." Challenge children to put on a "true" live puppet show of truth-telling situations.

THOUGHT TREAT: Write "I Chews to Tell the Truth" on Chewing Gum. As you chew, watch mouths open to tell the truth.

HONESTY Helps Me Follow the Straight and Narrow Path
(Step Toward Heaven Game)

YOU'LL NEED: Copies of wordstrips (page 59) and scissors

AGES 8-TEEN ACTIVITY: Read D&C 3:2 and talk about following in the steps of Jesus toward heaven, that straight and narrow path that leads to eternal life. If we get off the path, we need to be honest with ourselves and get back on, repent, and STEP TOWARD HEAVEN. Let's play the game. (1) Cut up and place wordstrips in a bowl and have family divide wordstrips equally. (2) Start at one side of the room with the goal to get to heaven (the other side of the room). (3) Take turns reading your wordstrips and stepping forward (if it is an honest choice or BONUS) or backwards (if it is a dishonest choice). (4) First one to heaven wins!

And they were also distinguished for their zeal towards God, and also towards men; for they were perfectly honest and upright in all things; and they were firm in the faith of Christ, even unto the end.

Alma 27:27

PATTERN: *HONESTY (smile and frown hand puppet)*

PATTERN: *TRUTH (Trevor Truth sack puppet)*

Trevor Truth

I can be strong and tell the truth!

PATTERN: *TRUTH (Trina Truth sack puppet)*

I can be strong and tell the truth!

Truth Trina

The man at the store gave me some extra change. I figured it was his mistake and I left without saying anything. . . . . .Honest or Dishonest?	I was taking a test and went up to sharpen my pencil. I took the chance, and looked over at Rick's test paper. . . . . Honest or Dishonest?
At the jewelry store, I saw a woman put a necklace in her pocket. I looked the other way and soon left. . . . . Honest or Dishonest?	My friend works at a department store. She gets an employee discount. She said I could buy with her discount anytime. Now I go to my friend and save money each time I shop. . . . .Honest or Dishonest?
In our town, Christmas trees are free if you cut your own. I saw the tree lot had plenty, so I took a free one. . . . . .Honest or Dishonest?	I really like to watch movies, and I get bored with the same old shows, so I borrowed some from a friend without asking. . . . . . .Honest or Dishonest?
I didn't study like I should for the test today. I was tempted to look on John's paper, but I resisted. . . . . Honest or Dishonest?	I really like to visit my mom's sister. She is fun, and tells me she likes my visits. I let her know that I really enjoy visiting. . . Honest or Dishonest?
I went to the zoo today and bought some peanuts to feed the elephant. I received too much change, so I returned the money before feeding the elephant. . . . . Honest or Dishonest?	My friend likes to tell things that aren't true. I told her that it's not a good idea, but she still talks about others. I decided to walk away next time so I don't have to listen. . . . . Honest or Dishonest?
I went to a friend's house for dinner. His mother made us dinner, and I don't like brussels sprouts. Instead of saying I didn't want any, I ate them and almost threw up. . . . . Honest or Dishonest?	When my parents are not at home, my friends want to watch movies that aren't good. I tell them that I don't want to and suggest movies I feel good about. . . . . Honest or Dishonest?
I take my time each Sunday getting ready for church. I make my family late. They miss the sacrament in sacrament meeting. . . . . Honest or Dishonest?	I lost my Book of Mormon. My mom gave me some money and told me to go to the bookstore and buy me a new one. I went to the store and bought a video. . . . . Honest or Dishonest?
Your parents are gone, and they said you had to be home from your friend's house at 10:00. You came home at 11:00. . . . . Honest or Dishonest?	My friend wanted to go to the store instead of straight home from school. Mom said to come straight home, so I said, "No, let's go home and have mother drive us there." Honest or Dishonest?
My teacher at school does things that bug me. I am tempted to tell my friends about her. Instead, I try to work it out or talk to my parents. . . . . Honest or Dishonest?	I went to a fast food place and ordered two cheese burgers and a shake. When I was eating I thought, what a good deal, two burgers for the price of one. Then I found out I shortchanged them. So I pulled out some extra cash. . . . . . . .Honest or Dishonest?
BONUS: I was honest all day! . . . . MOVE AHEAD THREE.	In baseball I said the ball didn't touch me, but it did. It looked like my team was going to win, so I had to tell. . . . . Honest or Dishonest?
BONUS: I wasn't late. . . . . MOVE AHEAD ONE.	BONUS: I told my sister I was sorry. . . . . MOVE AHEAD TWO.
BONUS: My friend was talking bad about someone and I said I didn't agree. . . . . MOVE AHEAD TWO.	Dad asked me if I had read my scriptures. I said said, "yes," when the answer was really no. . . . . Honest or Dishonest?

OBEDIENCE *Brings Blessings*

PREPARE AHEAD: Scripture Lesson, Bite-size Memorize Poster, Activity, and Thought Treat

OPENING SONG/PRAYER: "Choose the Right Way," page 160, Children's Songbook*

BITE-SIZE MEMORIZE: Present the D&C 82:10 poster (shown right) on page 63. Color poster and display to learn.

SCRIPTURE LESSON: Search and ponder scriptures below and on the following page.

BITE-SIZE MEMORIZE

I, the Lord, am bound when ye do what I say; but when ye do not what I say ye have no promise.

D&C 82:10

OBEDIENCE *Brings Blessings*

"Learn in thy youth to keep the commandments ..." and you will be *"lifted up at the last day."*
. . . . Alma 37:35-37
BLESSINGS COME AFTER OBEDIENCE TO COMMANDMENTS (D&C 130:18-21; 132:5; 53:7):
♥ *"Fulness of the earth is yours."* . . . . D&C 59:15-20, Deuteronomy 6:18
♥ Be added upon, receiving blessings forever . . . . Abraham 3:25-26, Mosiah 2:41, Mosiah 2:24
♥ Have eternal life, *"the greatest of all the gifts of God."* . . . . D&C 14:7, 2 Nephi 31:20
♥ Filled with joy and love . . . . Mosiah 2:41, John 13:17, Proverbs 29:18
HOW TO OBEY THE COMMANDMENTS (Jeremiah 7:23-24, Abraham 3:25):
♥ Pray and Choose The Right . . . D&C 68:28, Isaiah 55:6, 3 Nephi 17:21, Alma 13:28-29, Alma 30:8
♥ Follow Jesus . . . . Matthew 3:13-16, 3 Nephi 17:11-12, John 14:21
♥ Obey the Lord . . . . . . 1 Nephi 3:1-7, and sing "Nephi's Courage," page 120 Children's Songbook*
♥ Obey your parents . . . . Exodus 20:12, Mosiah 13:20, Colossians 3:20
♥ Obey the Ten Commandments . . . . Mosiah 12:32-37, D&C 42:18-28, Exodus 20:3-17
♥ Love others . . . . . D&C 59:5, Moses 6:33, D&C 42:29, D&C 4:2-4, Matthew 22:36-40, D&C 59:6
♥ Attend church meetings . . . . D&C 59:9, 12
♥ Fast and pray . . . . D&C 59:14
♥ Prepare to go to the temple . . . . 1 Corinthians 3:16-17
♥ Increase faith in Jesus Christ, repent, be baptized, receive the Holy Ghost . . . Fourth Article of Faith
♥ Obey the laws of the land . . . . D&C 58:21, Alma 53:18-22
CONSEQUENCES OF DISOBEDIENCE . . . . Isaiah 60:12, D&C 1:14; 93:39; 132:6

HOME-SPUN FUN ACTIVITIES: Select activities from the following pages to make learning fun.

CLOSING SONG/PRAYER: "I Will Follow God's Plan," page 164 in Children's Songbook*

THOUGHT TREAT: Big "O" Doughnut to remind children to "O"bey.

MORE LESSON IDEAS: IDEA #1—*Gospel Principles** Chapter 35 (pages 223-228)
IDEA #2—Primary lessons found in the *Primary** manuals (see LESSON IDEAS, pages 61-62)
IDEA #3—*Family Home Evening Resource Book** (pages 11, 13)
IDEA #4—*Uniform System for Teaching the Gospel** missionary discussions #2 (pages 2-20, 21)
IDEA #5—*Book of Mormon Reader** "The Brass Plates," pages 21-25
IDEA #6—*Old Testament Stories** "Noah," pages 26-29, and "The Ten Commandments," pages 75-78

*Songbook and suggested lesson materials are published by The Church of Jesus Christ of Latter-day Saints, Salt Lake City, Utah.

OBEDIENCE *Activities and Lesson Ideas*

PARENTS: My Parents Help Me Learn the Commandments
(home slide-show)

LESSON IDEAS: See lesson #28 in Primary 3-CTR B manual*.

YOU'LL NEED: Copy of home and pull-through pictures (page 64) on colored cardstock paper for each child, scissors, glue, razor blade, and crayons

AGES 3-7 ACTIVITY: Show children ways their parents help them learn to obey the commandments with pull-through pictures.
1. Ahead of time, parents should cut out slits on both sides of door with a razor blade.
2. Color and cut out home and pull-through pictures.
3. Insert or slide through pictures
4. Fold back edges of picture to prevent pulling all the way out.

THOUGHT TREAT: <u>Graham Cracker House</u>. Create a house for each child. Frost four small graham crackers on sides (sticking sides together) to make a house. Talk about the family's house, what they learn inside the house, and how they obey the commandments.

OBEDIENCE: I Have "Bean" Obedient
(bean bag)

LESSON IDEAS: See lesson #28 in Primary 1 manual*.

YOU'LL NEED: Copy of beans and bean family label patterns (pages 65-66) on colored cardstock paper, a zip-close plastic sandwich bag for each child, scissors, and crayons

AGES 3-7 ACTIVITY: Play the "I Have 'Bean' Obedient" game with children using bean faces. Pull them out of the bag one at a time. Name the beans and ask each child how this bean has been obedient.
♥ <u>Lova Bean</u> shows love to friends and family,
♥ <u>Toya Bean</u> puts its toys away.
♥ <u>Beda Bean</u> makes its bed right away!
♥ <u>Keepa Bean</u> keeps the commandments.
♥ <u>Folda Bean</u> folds its arms,
♥ <u>Whispa Bean</u> whispers if baby is sleeping.
♥ <u>Quiet Bean</u> walks quietly at church.
1. Color and cut out beans and bean bag label.
2. Place bean bag label inside the bag, and then the beans.

THOUGHT TREAT: <u>Jelly Beans</u> inside bag to eat during family home evening, as you talk about each obedient bean.

OBEDIENCE *Activities and Lesson Ideas*

OBEDIENCE: Heavenly Father Will Help Me As I Obey
(message dangler)

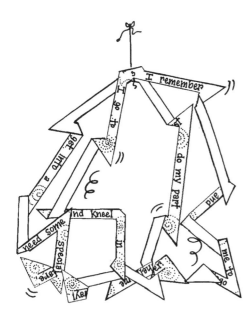

LESSON IDEA: See lesson #5 in Primary 5 manual*.

YOU'LL NEED: Copy of message dangler (page 67) on colored cardstock paper, and a 12" string, scissors, and crayons

AGES 8-11 ACTIVITY:
Read with children the message on the message dangler. This will help children know that as they obey Heavenly Father's commandments, they can ask him for help. Heavenly Father loves them and will help them find their way back to their heavenly home.

When I get into a fix
and need some special care,
I go to Heavenly Father
and kneel in humble prayer.
I remember that He loves me
and wants me to obey.
So I must do my part
and He'll help me find the way!

TO MAKE MESSAGE DANGLER: (1) Color message dangler. (2) Cut out dangler lines (unbroken). (3) Pierce a hole in the top with a pencil. (4) Tie a knot in a 12" string and thread through. (5) Children can hang dangler in their room. (6) Add glitter.

THOUGHT TREAT: Endure to the End Licorice. (1) Give each child a string of long licorice. (2) Enjoy eating licorice to the end of the rope as you talk about enduring to the end. Ask children what they want to be or to do with their life in the next five years and beyond. (3) Read D&C 14:7 and tell children that Heavenly Father wants us to endure to the end, and to obey his commandments every day of our lives.

OBEDIENCE: I Will Obey Heavenly Father Like Alma and Amulek
(missionary flip story)

LESSON IDEAS: See lesson #15 in Primary 4 manual*.

YOU'LL NEED: Copy of flip story pictures (page 68) on colored cardstock paper, and flip story cue cards #1-6 (page 69) on lightweight paper for each child, scissors, glue, paper punch, string, tape or page reinforcers, and crayons

AGES 8-TEEN ACTIVITY: Help children learn the importance of faithfully obeying Heavenly Father's commandments. Create a flip story to show how Alma and Amulek obeyed Heavenly Father and served their mission. See another Alma and Amulek flip story on pages 31, 38-39 (subject: Faith).

TO MAKE FLIP STORY: (1) Color and cut out picture cards #1-6. Cut out cue cards #1-6. (2) Glue cue cards #1-6 on backs of picture cards. Be sure to start gluing cue card #1 on the back of picture #6 (don't cut instructions off cue cards). (3) Tape over holes before punching holes, or punch holes and use page reinforcements. (4) Place string loosely through holes to make a flip chart.

I, the Lord, am bound when ye do what I say; but when ye do not what I say, ye have no promise.

D&C 82:10

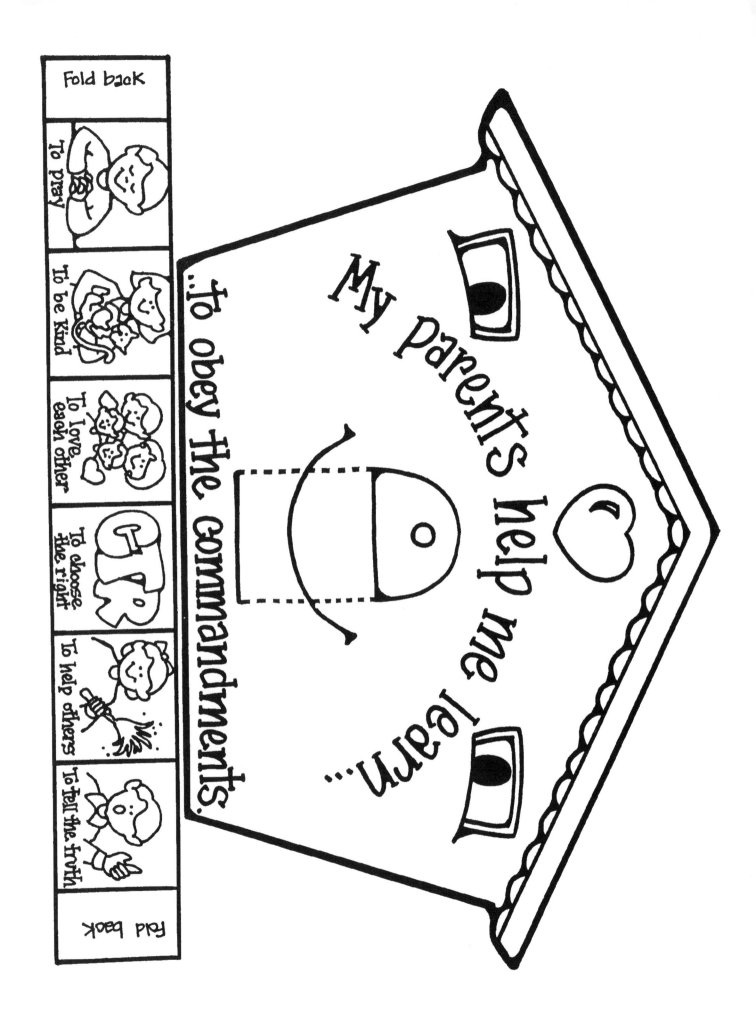

PATTERN: *OBEDIENCE (bean bag)*

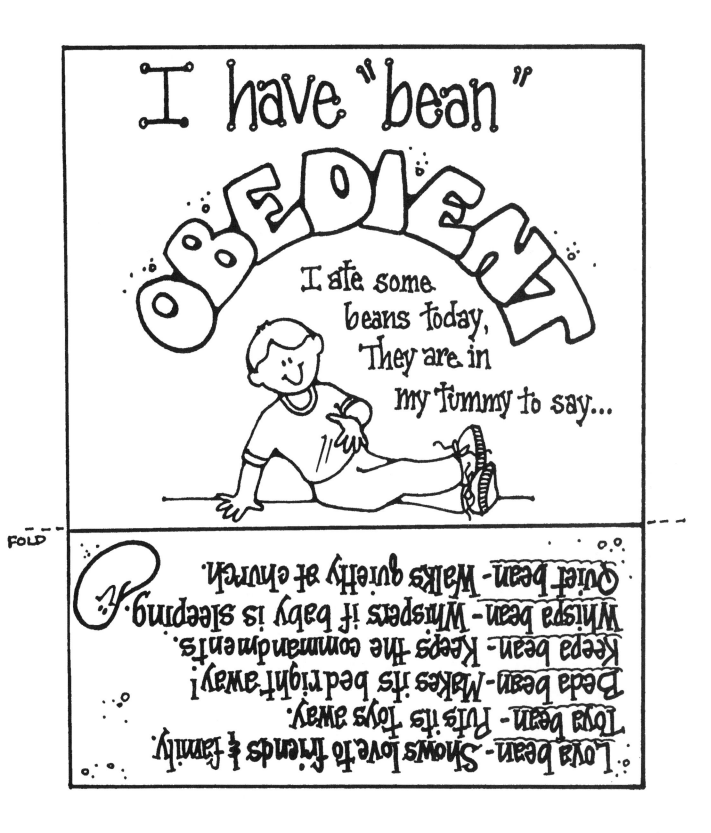

FOLD

PATTERN: *OBEDIENCE (beans to place in bean bag)*

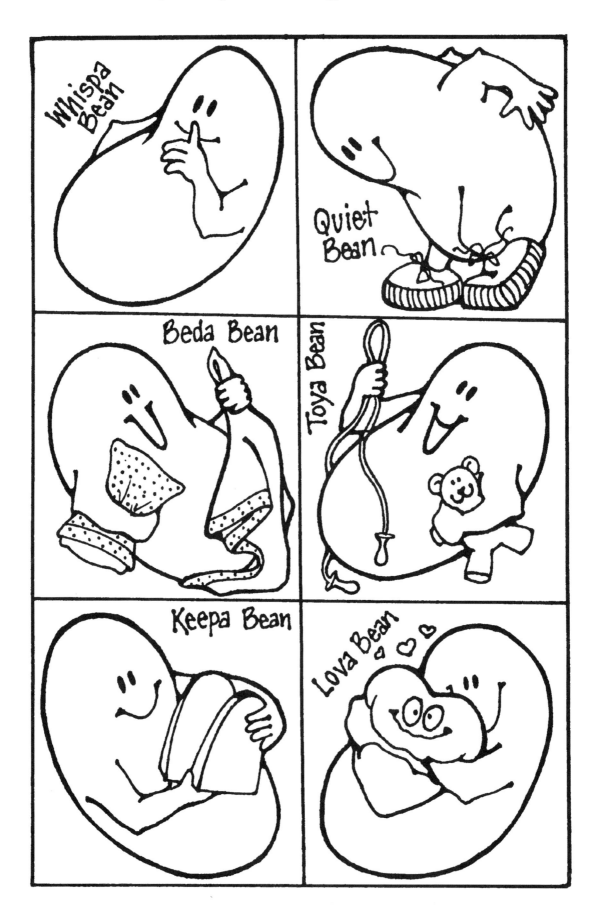

PATTERN: *OBEDIENCE (message dangler)*

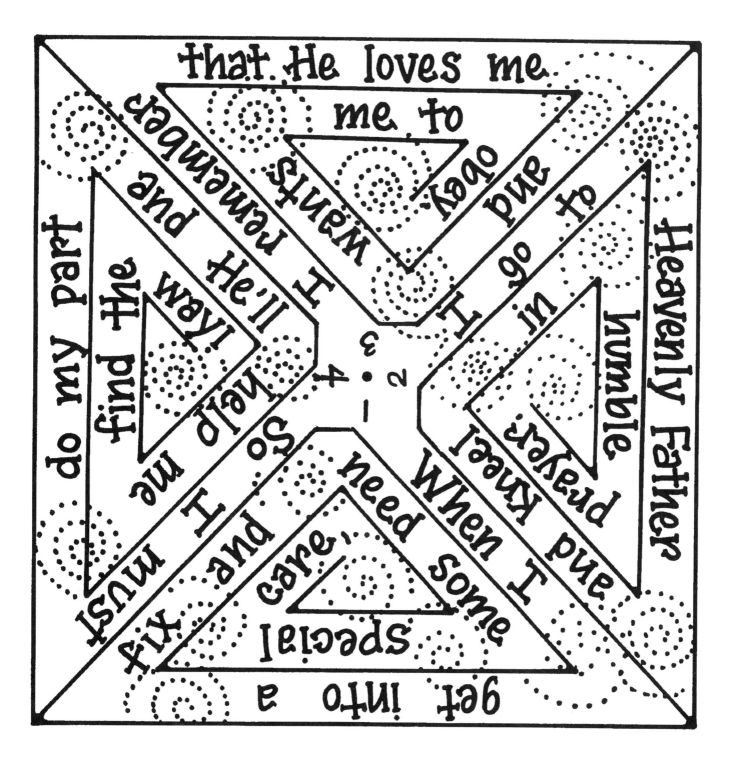

PATTERN: *OBEDIENCE (missionary flip story)*

PATTERN: *OBEDIENCE (missionary flip story)*

I Will Obey Heavenly Father

Alma the Younger was chosen by God to lead the Church. He went out to teach the people to obey God's commandments. The people from some cities repented, were baptized, and started to obey God's commandments.

CUE CARD #1 - Glue to back of picture card #6

But the people from Ammonihah would not listen. In Alma 8:9 we learn that Satan had gotten hold upon the hearts of the people in Ammonihah. They would not listen. They forced Alma to leave.

CUE CARD #2 - Glue to back of picture card #1

Alma the Younger felt sorrow for the people. An angel came to him saying, "Alma ... lift up thy head and rejoice ... for thou hast been faithful in keeping the commandments of God." The angel commanded him to return to Ammonihah to preach to the people, to tell them to repent, or they would be destroyed.

CUE CARD #3 - Glue to back of picture card #2

Alma the Younger went back to Ammonihah and met a righteous man named Amulek who gave him food. Amulek went with Alma the Younger and told the people to repent.

CUE CARD #4 - Glue to back of picture card #3

Zeezrom, a wicked man, tried to trick Amulek into saying something that was not true. But Alma and Amulek were filled with the Spirit and knew the thoughts and intents of his heart. Zeezrom knew he was wrong and asked Alma and Amulek to teach him.

CUE CARD #5 - Glue to back of picture card #4

Alma the Younger obeyed Heavenly Father in teaching the people. He shared his testimony with them.
I, too, can obey Heavenly Father and tell others about the gospel of Jesus Christ.

CUE CARD #6 - Glue to back of picture card #5

PRAYER: *I Will Pray to Keep Heaven Close*

PREPARE AHEAD: Scripture Lesson, Bite-size Memorize Poster, Activity, and Thought Treat

OPENING SONG/PRAYER: "A Child's Prayer," page 12 in the Children's Songbook*

BITE-SIZE MEMORIZE: Present the D&C 31:12 poster (shown right) on page 73. Color poster and display to learn.

SCRIPTURE LESSON: Search and ponder scriptures below.

PRAYER: *I Will Pray to Keep Heaven Close*

We are heaven sent and heaven bound. If we are to return to our heavenly home, let's pray, morning, noon and night to keep heaven in sight. . . . . .Psalm 55:17, Alma 34:21, D&C 138:56, Enos 1:27, Matthew 19:14

♥ PRAY for guidance. . . . . .Psalm 5:3, 12

♥ PRAY with humility. . . . . D&C 112:10, Alma 7:23

♥ PRAY with your heart . . . . Jeremiah 29:13, Psalm 14:2

♥ PRAY to stay close to Heavenly Father and Jesus Christ.   D&C 88:63, Alma 37:36-37, Psalm 104:34

♥ PRAY to know that God lives. . . . . Moroni 10:7

♥ PRAY to give thanks. . . . . .D&C 59:7; 136:28, Psalm 147:7-8; 100:4; 92:1-2

♥ PRAY for others. . . . . James 5:16

♥ PRAY in secret. . . . . .3 Nephi 13:5-8, Matthew 6:6

♥ PRAY to Father in Heaven in the name of Jesus Christ. . . . . . . .3 Nephi 13:15; 18:19, Mormon 9:27

♥ PRAY to avoid temptation. . . . . .3 Nephi 18:15-18, Alma 13:28-29

♥ PRAY with faith to receive blessings. . . .3 Nephi 18:20, D&C 11:12-14, Matthew 21:22, Mark 11:24

♥ PRAY with the family. . . . . 3 Nephi 18:21

♥ PRAY for wisdom and courage, having faith. . . . . .James 1:5-6

♥ PRAY for truth. . . . . .Moroni 10:4-5

♥ PRAY and fast for the welfare of others. . . . . Moroni 6:5

♥ PRAY to forgive others. . . . . Mark 11:25

♥ *"PRAY without ceasing."* . . . . 1 Thessalonians 5:17-23

♥ PRAY for strength. . . . . Psalm 105:4

♥ PRAYERS are always answered, "yes," "no," or "wait.". . . . . . . Matthew 7:11, D&C 88:64; 112:10

HOME-SPUN FUN ACTIVITIES: Select activities from the following pages to make learning fun.

CLOSING SONG/PRAYER: "I Know My Father Lives," page 5 in Children's Songbook*

THOUGHT TREAT: Prayer Punch. Talk about prayer as you sip your favorite punch. Say, "Prayer adds punch to our lives, it gives us energy, it is sweet, and it makes us feel good as we talk to our Heavenly Father."

MORE LESSON IDEAS: IDEA #1—*Gospel Principles** pages 41-45, 356—Song: *"Did You Think to Pray?"*
IDEA #2—Primary lessons found in the *Primary** manuals (see LESSON IDEAS on page 71-72)
IDEA #3—*Family Home Evening Resource Book** (pages 27-30, 80-83, 139)
IDEA #4—*Uniform System for Teaching the Gospel** missionary Instructions for Discussions (page 8)
IDEA #5—*Book of Mormon Reader** "Jesus Comes to America," page 92 . .   3 Nephi 13:6-13; 18:15-24
IDEA #6—*New Testament Stories** "Prayer," page 51—Matthew 6:5-8; 6:9-13; John 16:23, Luke 11:5-10

*Songbook and suggested lesson materials are published by The Church of Jesus Christ of Latter-day Saints, Salt Lake City, Utah.

PRAYER *Activities and Lesson Ideas*

PRAYER: To Heavenly Father I Will Pray
(Daniel and lions' den drama scene)

LESSON IDEAS: See lesson #4 in Primary 1 manual*.

YOU'LL NEED: Copy Daniel, den, and lions (page 74) on tan cardstock paper for each child, scissors, and crayons

AGES 8-7 ACTIVITY: Create Daniel and lions' den to help children act out the scene where Daniel prayed to Heavenly Father. Then the lions did not eat Daniel. Read: *Old Testament Stories** "Daniel and the Lions' Den," pages 156-157 - Daniel 6:1-23

PRAYER: I Like to Pray with My Family
(family prayer fan)

LESSON IDEAS: See lesson #27 in Primary 1 manual*.

YOU'LL NEED: Copy of fan (page 75) on colored lightweight paper for each child, yarn or ribbon, scissors, paper punch, and crayons

AGES 3-7 ACTIVITY: Create a family prayer fan to show children that Heavenly Father wants us to pray with our family every day. You will receive many blessings as you pray with your family. (1) Color and cut out fan. (2) Fan-fold paper into a fan. (3) Punch a hole at the bottom of the fan and tie yarn or ribbon through hole to hold fan together.

PRAYER: Heavenly Father Hears and Answers My Prayers
("YES," "NO" wristbands)

LESSON IDEAS: See lesson #18 in Primary 2-CTR A manual*.

YOU'LL NEED: Copy of "YES" and "NO" wristbands (page 76) on colored cardstock paper and two 1/2" pieces sticky-back Velcro or tape for each child, scissors, and crayons

AGES 8-11 ACTIVITY: Create "YES" and "NO" wristbands children can wear on each wrist to help them make decisions that are best. This will help them judge how Heavenly Father might answer their prayer. The "YES" wristband reads: "YES because it's OK," and the "NO" wristband reads: "NO because it is best for me."

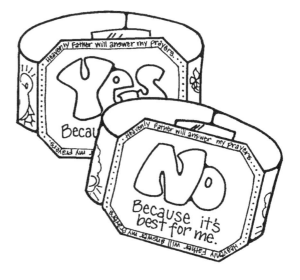

SITUATIONS TO DISCUSS: The lesson* suggests several parent and child situations. Here are a few more.
1. Your child wants his dinner, but the dog is hungry too. Do you feed him his dinner first? "NO." Why do you say that?
2. Your child wants to run out on the icy, slippery porch. Do you let him? "NO." Why do you say that?
3. The work is done and it's time for fun. Do you go to the park? "YES." Why did you say that?
4. Your child needs his sleep and it's time to go to bed. He still wants to play. "NO." Why do you say that?
5. The fish tank is dirty. Do you let your fish swim in dirty water? "NO." Why do you say that?
6. Aunt Nedra is sick and needs some loving care. Do you leave? "NO." Why did you say that?
7. Your child's favorite TV show is on. Did you help first by setting the table? "YES." Why did you say that?
HOW TO VOTE: Tell children they must listen carefully and only say "YES" or "NO" to the answers. When they hear "YES" they are to raise their "YES" wristband. When they hear "NO" they raise their "NO" wristband.

PRAYER *Activities and Lesson Ideas*

PRAY: I Can Pray to Heavenly Father and Jesus
(Monday through Sunday prayer elevator)

LESSON IDEAS: See lesson #34 in Primary 3-CTR B manual*.

YOU'LL NEED: Copy of paper doll child praying and elevator (page 77) on colored cardstock paper, scissors, glue, tape, and crayons

AGES 6-11 ACTIVITY: To encourage children to pray to Heavenly Father as Jesus did, create an elevator where child can pray each day, Monday - Sunday. Child pulls the string or ribbon to pull the paper doll child up the elevator seven times (once daily) to get the full message written on the fan: "I grow each day when I pray ... closer to Heavenly Father."
(1) Color and cut out elevator, child praying, and wordstrip. (2) Glue head on wordstrip where indicated. (3) Cut slits in top and bottom of the elevator. (4) Thread strip through top and bottom slits in elevator with head at the top. (5) Tape or glue strip ends together where indicated so strip will move freely. (6) Move child arrow to first day, then down to reveal message at the end of the week.
THOUGHT TREAT: <u>Monday-Sunday Mints</u>. Give each child 7 small butter mints one at a time. As mints melt in their mouth, ask them to say the days of the week. Then say, "Heavenly Father and Jesus wants us ("mint" for us) to pray every day of the week—Monday, Tuesday, Wednesday," etc.

PRAYER: I Will Seek Heavenly Father's Guidance
(prayer crossword puzzle)

LESSON IDEAS: See lesson #6 in Primary 5 manual*.

YOU'LL NEED: Copy of prayer crossword puzzle (page 78) on colored cardstock paper, and a pencil for each child, and crayons

AGES 8-11 ACTIVITY: Complete this prayer crossword puzzle together to show children that answers to prayers come in many ways.
ANSWER KEY: <u>ACROSS:</u> 5—Heavenly Father, 7—ask, 8—morning, 9—listen, 10—thank, 15—still small voice, 17—help. <u>DOWN:</u> 1—Holy Ghost, 2—prayer, 3—Jesus Christ, 4—yes, 6—guidance, 11—knees, 12—night, 13—blessings, 14—no, 18—peace.
THOUGHT TREAT: <u>Prayer Popcorn</u>. Provide a bowl of popcorn children can munch on. Each time they take a handful, they can tell something they might ask Heavenly Father for or thank him for. Tell children that just as <u>heat warms</u> kernels of corn before they pop, <u>prayer warms</u> our heart, and messages from the Holy Ghost can "pop" into our mind.

PRAYER Will Protect Me from Temptation
(Then and Now Challenges obstacle course game)

LESSON IDEAS: See lesson #37 in Primary 4 manual*.

YOU'LL NEED: Copy of board game, cards, and Team #1 and #2 markers (pages 79-82) on colored cardstock paper, scissors, glue, crayons, and die (two dice)

AGES 8-TEENS ACTIVITY: Play the game that teaches children about prayer THEN: in NEPHITE ZION, and NOW: TODAY'S ZION. The game will take you to these two time periods.
TO MAKE GAME: Color and cut out game board parts A and B, cards, and markers. Glue parts A and B together.
TO PLAY: See instructions on page 82.

PATTERN: *PRAYER (Daniel and lions' den drama scene)*

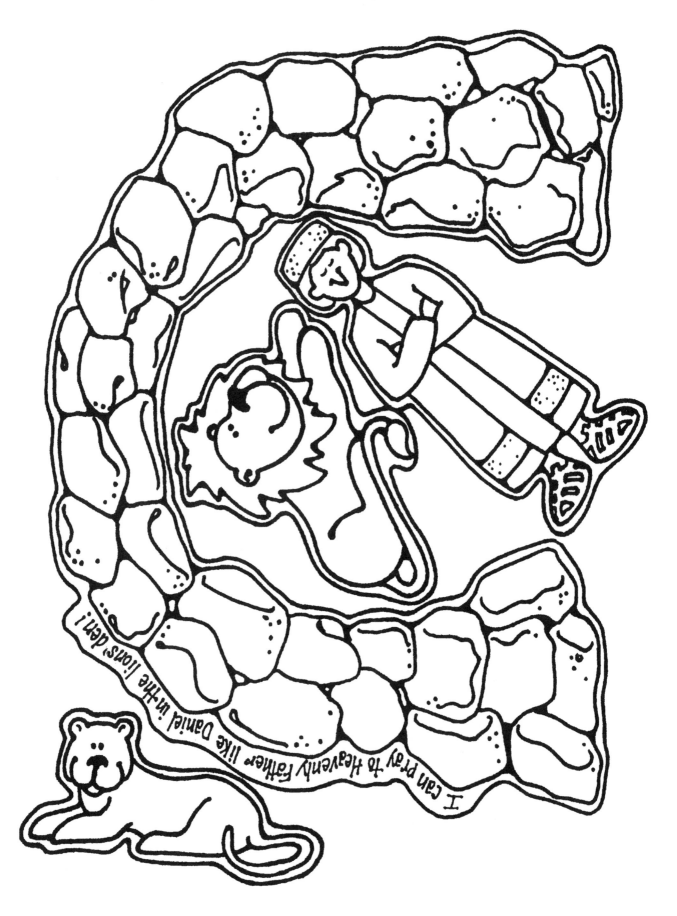

I can pray to Heavenly Father like Daniel in the lions' den!

PATTERN: *PRAYER ("YES," "NO" wristbands)*

PATTERN: *PRAYER (Monday through Sunday prayer elevator)*

Elevator Prayer Chart

Monday
Tuesday
Wednesday
Thursday
Friday
Saturday
Sunday

Glue B here

I grow each day when I pray to Heavenly Father.

Glue A here

A
B

A
B

Puzzled about Prayer?

ACROSS
5. a parent (2 words)
7. request
8. early day
9. to hear
10. show gratitude
15. speaks to heart and mind (3 words)
17. aid

DOWN
1. invisible friend
2. kneeling activity
3. elder brother
4. affirmative
6. direction
11. prayer bones
12. day's companion
13. count them
14. negative
16. the last word
18. war's opposite

PATTERN: *PRAYER (Then and Now Challenges obstacle course game)*

STUMBLING BLOCK (THEN & NOW): It's time to get up in the morning and you think of that saying, "Early to bed, early to rise, makes one healthy, wealthy, and wise," but you're tired. WHAT WOULD YOU PRAY ABOUT?	**STUMBLING BLOCK** (THEN): You wanted to go with your friends and build a tree house, but your brother has asked you to help him build a boat to sail to the Promised Land. WHAT WOULD YOU PRAY ABOUT?	**STUMBLING BLOCK** (THEN): You are told by the Lord to build a boat without any windows. You wonder how you can sail without light. WHAT WOULD YOU PRAY ABOUT?
STUMBLING BLOCK (THEN): It's been known for a while that a bright star will shine when Jesus Christ is born. Do you believe what they are saying is true? WHAT WOULD YOU PRAY ABOUT?	**STUMBLING BLOCK** (THEN & NOW): The prophet was telling you to believe in Jesus Christ, and your friends told you to trust in your own thoughts. WHAT WOULD YOU PRAY ABOUT?	**STUMBLING BLOCK** (THEN & NOW): There are others around you who are not living the commandments. They want you to be a part of their plans. You can see that they are becoming more and more wicked. WHAT WOULD YOU PRAY ABOUT?
STUMBLING BLOCK (THEN & NOW): You were asked by the Lord and the prophet to keep a record or journal of your people, and you did not know what to write about. WHAT WOULD YOU PRAY ABOUT?	**STUMBLING BLOCK** (THEN): You are searching for the way to heaven, and others tell you it is found by climbing there. They ask you to help them build a tower. WHAT WOULD YOU PRAY ABOUT?	**STUMBLING BLOCK** (THEN): You are around people who want to fight and kill others. They want you to join their army to take over their enemy's land. WHAT WOULD YOU PRAY ABOUT?
STUMBLING BLOCK (THEN & NOW): Your parents asked you to take care of the house while they are gone. They want you to water the garden and plants and take care of the animals. You are there alone now. WHAT WOULD YOU PRAY ABOUT?	**STUMBLING BLOCK** (THEN & NOW): You are asked to leave your home and leave all the things that you own. You are asked to take your sleeping bag and survival needs. You are asked to do this because your father asked you to. WHAT WOULD YOU PRAY ABOUT?	**STUMBLING BLOCK** (THEN): You were asked to get something from a wicked man, a genealogy, a sacred record that was important to your family. You hesitate, because you don't know if you will come back alive. WHAT WOULD YOU PRAY ABOUT?
STUMBLING BLOCK (THEN & NOW): Your brothers do not listen to the prophet and the words which are in the scriptures. They would rather go their own way and do what they want to do. You want to listen to the prophet and live the commandments. WHAT WOULD YOU PRAY ABOUT?	**STUMBLING BLOCK** (THEN & NOW): Your parents take you to live in a place you have never been. You don't know anyone, and you are not sure you want to live there. You have left all your friends, and you would like to run back to where you came from. WHAT WOULD YOU PRAY ABOUT?	**STUMBLING BLOCK** (THEN & NOW): You have gained knowledge of the scriptures and you know the teachings of Jesus Christ are true. Your friend does not know what you know, and starts asking you questions about what you believe. WHAT WOULD YOU PRAY ABOUT?
STUMBLING BLOCK (THEN & NOW): You haven't been living the teachings of Jesus, and you want your friends to disobey the commandments with you. You have a strong feeling that if you don't repent now, you will never find the truth. WHAT WOULD YOU PRAY ABOUT?	**STUMBLING BLOCK** (THEN & NOW): You know it's time for you to go on a mission and start telling others about the gospel of Jesus Christ. You want to tell others about the gospel, but you are not sure if the words you speak are right. You are afraid that people will laugh at the way you say things. WHAT WOULD YOU PRAY ABOUT?	**STUMBLING BLOCK** (THEN & NOW): Someone needs your help. You ask them what you can do to help, and do it without pay. You are beginning to build a friendship. This person is beginning to trust you and want you for a friend. You feel it's time to talk about the gospel, but you wait. WHAT WOULD YOU PRAY ABOUT?

BLESSING BONUS:	BLESSING BONUS:	BLESSING BONUS:
You went the extra mile today. You stopped, you looked, you listened, and you did obey. MOVE FORWARD ONE STEP.	You've done a lot of work, you did not shirk, you put your shoulder to the wheel. Ask the members of your team to yell, "HIP HIP HOORAY!"	Blessings are in store forever more because you are a faithful Saint. Take each blessing one by one and count what God has done. BEGIN COUNTING!
BLESSING BONUS: Your mother is a dear, she gives you lots of cheer. You deserve the best, so give your mother some rest and SAY MOTHER DEAR, I LOVE YOU!	**BLESSING BONUS:** Blessings unnumbered await you today, as you have chosen the righteous way. CONSIDER YOURSELF BLESSED!	**BLESSING BONUS:** Look at what you've got, not what you have not. Look at those who are less fortunate than you and decide just what you can do to help. MAKE A LIST.
BLESSING BONUS: It's about time you found the time to tell yourself that you are terrific! Say it now! "I'M TERRIF!" MOVE AHEAD ONE.	**BLESSING BONUS:** Not one, not two, but eternal blessings true. They wait for you as you pursue...living the gospel of Jesus Christ. MOVE AHEAD ONE.	**BLESSING BONUS:** If you want to move forward in this game, just name it, you can choose. Roll the dice and move any number between 1 and 4. ROLL DICE AND MOVE.
BLESSING BONUS: Ever since you were in the crib, you wanted to say, "goo goo," so say it now while you have an audience true! "GOO GOO DA DA MA MA!" MOVE AHEAD ONE SPACE.	**BLESSING BONUS:** Farewell to troubles, farewell to gloom, you have entered the happiness room. Each time you pray you can say you chose the righteous way. Say "Amen," and MOVE AHEAD ONE. AMEN.	**BLESSING BONUS:** As you are living the teachings of the living prophet—having family home evening, reading scriptures, having family and personal prayers, paying tithing, and attending church—MOVE AHEAD TWO.
BLESSING BONUS: It's no joke, you are not a slowpoke. You sped on past the other guys in your class! MOVE AHEAD TWO SPACES.	**BLESSING BONUS:** Give me a nickel, give me a dime, money means nothing when it's going to heaven time! You can't take earthly treasures with you, so dig deep for heavenly treasures that are safe to keep. MOVE AHEAD FOUR SPACES.	**BLESSING BONUS:** For praying with an honest heart and doing your best to do your part, MOVE AHEAD TWO SPACES.
BLESSING BONUS: Blessing Bonanza! The Book of Mormon tells of people who were blessed when they were righteous. They prayed, lived the commandments, and really made the grade! For living like the righteous Nephites and Lamanites, MOVE ONE.	**BLESSING BONUS:** Think of THEN in Book of Mormon times and think of NOW and how you're blessed, and how! Name one of your blessings and MOVE AHEAD ONE.	**BLESSING BONUS:** You want to win, your team is pushing ahead. Take a deep breath and MOVE AHEAD TWO SPACES!.

THEN & NOW CHALLENGES GAME

HOW TO PLAY: ♥ Put Stumbling Block cards and Blessing Bonus cards face down in separate piles. ♥ Divide players into two teams or play individually. Place marker on board at START. Take turns rolling die and moving marker on board toward HEAVEN. ♥ Draw a Stumbling Block card when you land on SB. Answer what you would pray about to make a decision living THEN in Nephite Zion or NOW in Today's Zion. ♥ Draw a Blessing Bonus card when you land on BB (move or do as it says). ♥ First one to reach HEAVEN wins! Or, play until all cards are read.

PRIESTHOOD: *Special Power to Guide and Bless Me*

PREPARE AHEAD: Scripture Lesson, Bite-size Memorize Poster, Activity, and Thought Treat
OPENING SONG/PRAYER: "The Priesthood Is Restored," page 89, Children's Songbook*
BITE-SIZE MEMORIZE: Present the D&C 121:36 poster (shown right) on page 86. Color poster and display to learn.
SCRIPTURE LESSON: Search and ponder scriptures below.

BITE-SIZE MEMORIZE
...The rights of the priesthood are inseparably connected with the powers of heaven, and that the powers of heaven cannot be controlled nor handled only upon the principles of righteousness. D&C 121:36

PRIESTHOOD: *Special Power to Guide and Bless Me*

♥ PRIESTHOOD is the power and authority of God given to worthy men for a great purpose. . . . . .Moses 1:39, Articles of Faith 1:5
♥ PRIESTHOOD men are called of God. . . Hebrews 5:4, Exodus 28:1
♥ PRIESTHOOD performs sacred gospel ordinances: baptism, confirmation, administration of the sacrament, and temple marriage. .Matthew 7:21-22
♥ PRIESTHOOD was given to man to act in God's name. . . . . .Mark 3:13-15; John 15:16
♥ PRIESTHOOD in latter days was revealed to the prophet Joseph Smith. . . . . .D&C 107:1-100
♥ PRIESTHOOD power cannot be bought or sold. .Acts 8:9-20
♥ PRIESTHOOD power can only be used in righteousness. . . . . .D&C 121:36-37, 41-44
♥ PRIESTHOOD can bless families. .D&C 121:41
♥ PRIESTHOOD power is connected to heaven. . . . . D&C 121:34-40
♥ PRIESTHOOD members need power of Holy Ghost. . . . . .D&C 121:45-46
♥ PRIESTHOOD in early church. . .D&C 68:12; 107:2-4, Alma 13:1-19, Hebrews 7:11-13, Matt. 16:19
♥ PRIESTHOOD duties are explained. . . . . .D&C 20:38-67, 1 Corinthians 12:14-31
♥ PRIESTHOOD leader is President of the Church, presiding high priest. . . . . .D&C 107:65-67
♥ PRIESTHOOD—Aaronic Priesthood in charge of temporal matters. . . . . .D&C 107:68, Positions: Teacher—age 14 or older (D&C 20:53-59; 42:12), Priest—age 16 or older (D&C 20:46-51), Bishop presides over Aaronic Priesthood (D&C 107:87-88), Aaronic Priesthood quorum consists of up to: 12 Deacons—D&C 107:85, 24 Teachers—D&C 107:86, and 48 priests—D&C 107:87-88
♥ PRIESTHOOD—Melchizedek Priesthood in charge of spiritual work. . . . . .D&C 84:19-22, Positions: Elder (D&C 20:42-45, 70; 46:2; 107:11), High Priest (D&C 68:19; 107:10, 12), Patriarch (D&C 107:39-56), Seventy (D&C 107:25, 34, 38, 93-97), Apostle (D&C 107:23) Melchizedek Priesthood quorum consists of Elders (D&C 124:137) and High Priests.
FUN ACTIVITIES: Select activities from the following pages to make learning fun.
CLOSING SONG/PRAYER: "Love Is Spoken Here," page 190 in the Children's Songbook*
THOUGHT TREAT: Priesthood Pretzels. Serve one for each office of the priesthood.
MORE LESSON IDEAS: IDEA #1—*Gospel Principles** Chapter 13 and 14
IDEA #2—Primary lessons found in the *Primary** manuals (see LESSON IDEAS, pages 84-85)
IDEA #3—*Family Home Evening Resource Book** (pages 84-88, 124-126)
IDEA #4—*Uniform System for Teaching the Gospel** missionary discussions #3 (pages 3-6, 3-10)
IDEA #5—*Doctrine and Covenants Stories** "Joseph and Oliver Are Given the Priesthood," pages 26-30
IDEA #6—*New Testament Stories** "Jesus Commands the Wind and the Waves," pages 56-57 (Luke 8)

*Songbook and suggested lesson materials are published by The Church of Jesus Christ of Latter-day Saints, Salt Lake City, Utah.

PRIESTHOOD *Activities and Lesson Ideas*

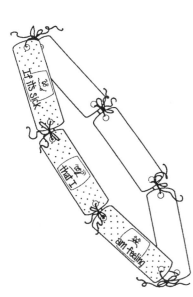

PRIESTHOOD BLESSINGS: The Priesthood Heals
(band-aid bandelo)

LESSON IDEAS: See lesson #16 in Primary 2-CTR A manual*.

YOU'LL NEED: Copy of band-aid bandelo (page 87) on colored cardstock paper and yarn or ribbon for each child, scissors, paper punch, and crayons

AGES 3-7 ACTIVITY: Create a huge bandelo that reads: "If it's sick that I am feeling, the priesthood can do the healing." Tell children that Jesus Christ has the power to heal and has given the priesthood to us to help heal the sick. (1) Color and cut out band-aid bandelo strips. (2) Paper punch holes at each end. (3) Tie yarn or ribbon to connect ends. (4) Place a band-aid bandelo around each child's shoulder to cross over the chest.

THOUGHT TREAT: <u>Choice #1: Bandage-shaped Wafer Cookie</u>. Decorate a frosted smile in the center of each bandage-shaped wafer cookie. <u>Choice #2: Smarties® or Candy-like Pills</u>. Tell children that pills are not candy. <u>Choice #3: Bandage Sandwiches</u>. Make sandwiches and cut bread into bandage-width strips.

PRIESTHOOD Blessings and Ordinances *(spiral kite to fly)*

LESSON IDEAS: See lesson #9 in Primary 3-CTR B manual*.

YOU'LL NEED: Copy of spiral kite (page 88) on colored cardstock paper, and 12" yarn or ribbon for each child, scissors, and crayons

AGES 5-8 ACTIVITY: To help children know that the priesthood is a special power to give blessings and perform ordinances such as baptism and healing of the sick. Create a spiral kite that tells of this power. Take hold of string and move arms to watch spiral kite twirl. (1) Color and cut out spiral kite. (2) Poke a hole in the center spot indicated. (3) Tie 12" yarn or ribbon through hole and fly!

PRIESTHOOD Can Help Me
(Priesthood Power Calmed Seas moving ship scene)

LESSON IDEAS: See lesson #17 in Primary 2-CTR A manual*.

YOU'LL NEED: Copy of moving ship scene and boat (pages 89-90) on colored cardstock paper and a wooden craft stick for each child, scissors, tape, and crayons

AGES 3-7 ACTIVITY: Create a moving ship scene to remind children of the scripture in Mark 4:39 where Jesus calmed the storm. This is to remind them that Jesus helps and blesses us through the power of the priesthood. (1) Color and cut out ship scene and boat. (2) Glue boat on half of the wooden craft stick. (3) Cut out handle and fold back tabs. Glue or tape handle to back of scene. (4) Cut hole where indicated by dotted line and insert boat on stick. Move the boat back and forth to simulate a rough sea. Then move more slowly to simulate a calm sea.

THOUGHT TREAT: <u>Banana Boat with Cheese Sails</u>. Cut a banana in half crosswise and lengthwise and insert a slice of cheese with a toothpick for the sail. As you eat, talk about the story from Mark 4:35-41.

*Primary manuals are published by The Church of Jesus Christ of Latter-day Saints, Salt Lake City, Utah.

PRIESTHOOD *Activities and Lesson Ideas*

PRIESTHOOD: The Special Power to Guide and Bless Us
(plug into Priesthood Power Lines)

LESSON IDEAS: See lesson #30 in Primary 4 manual*.

YOU'LL NEED: Copy of Priesthood Power Line activity (page 91) for each child, pens, and crayons
AGES 8-TEEN: Help children plug into Priesthood Power Lines by writing initials on the plug showing the duties, e.g. PE = Priest and Elder can bless the sacrament.
PRIESTHOOD DUTIES: ♥ A <u>DEACON</u>, at age 12, can hold the Aaronic Priesthood, pass the sacrament, act as a messenger for priesthood leaders, collect fast offerings, and care for church buildings and grounds. ♥ A <u>TEACHER</u>, at age 14, can hold the Aaronic Priesthood, perform all duties of a deacon, prepare bread and water for the sacrament, and be assigned to be a home teacher.
♥ A <u>PRIEST</u>, at age 16, can hold the Aaronic Priesthood, perform all duties of deacon and teacher, administer and bless the sacrament, and baptize. ♥ An <u>ELDER</u>, at age 18, can hold the Melchizedek Priesthood, may serve a full-time mission, watch over the Church, give the gift of the Holy Ghost, conduct meetings, bless children, administer to the sick, and bless family members.

PRIESTHOOD KEYS Unlock the Powers of Heaven
(priesthood keys doorknob reminder)

LESSON IDEAS: See lesson #26 in Primary 5 manual*.

YOU'LL NEED: Copy of keys pieces (page 92) on colored cardstock paper, and a 12" string for each child, scissors, and crayons
AGES 8-TEENS ACTIVITY: Remind children that Joseph Smith and Oliver Cowdery unlocked the powers of heaven when they received the priesthood keys from the prophets Moses and Elijah.
TO MAKE KEYS: (1) Read the scriptures on each key to know who restored which priesthood key, Moses or Elijah. (2) Cut out the Moses and Elijah figures and glue on the right key. (3) Glue keys back-to-back. (4) Punch a hole in key and tie a 12" string. Attach keys to your bedroom door to remind you of the priesthood keys that will unlock the powers of heaven.

PRIESTHOOD: Heavenly Keys
(priesthood keys crossword puzzle)

LESSON IDEAS: See lesson #15 in Primary 7 manual*.

YOU'LL NEED: Copy of crossword puzzle (page 93) on colored cardstock paper for each child, scissors, and crayons
AGES 8-TEEN ACTIVITY: Color and complete crossword puzzle. PARENT'S NOTE: Without telling the children, help them find the "Key" word "PRIESTHOOD" by completing the puzzle. Answers: Across 1—heal 4—blessing 6—priesthood 8—baptism
Down 1—Holy Ghost 2—temple 3—babies 5—name 7—sacrament

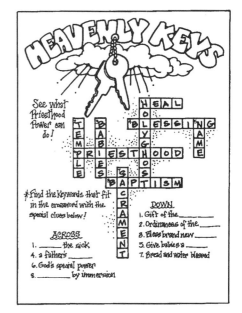

... The rights of the priesthood are inseparably connected with the powers of heaven, and that the powers of heaven cannot be controlled nor handled only upon the principles of righteousness. D&C 121:36

1. If it's sick
2. that I
3. am feeling
4. I'll let
5. the priesthood

do the healing

The Priesthood power calmed the seas.

Peace, be still.

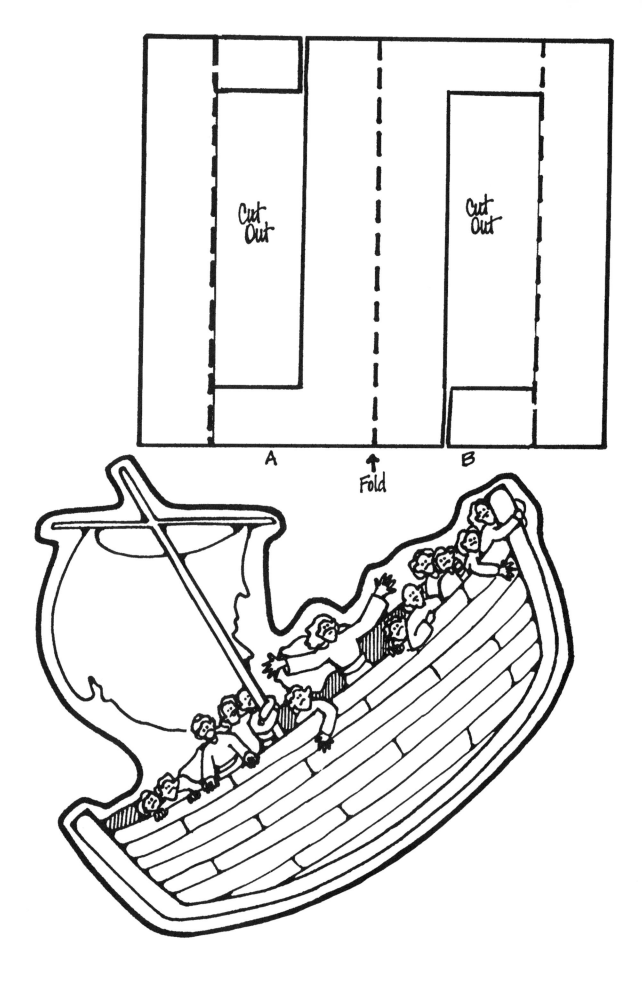

Cut Out

Cut Out

A

Fold

B

PATTERN: *PRIESTHOOD (keys doorknob reminder)*

D&C 110:13-16 Restored the keys of the sealing power so families can be together forever!

MOSES

ELIJAH

D&C 110:11 Restored the keys of the gathering of Israel so missionaries can bring people into the church!

HEAVENLY KEYS

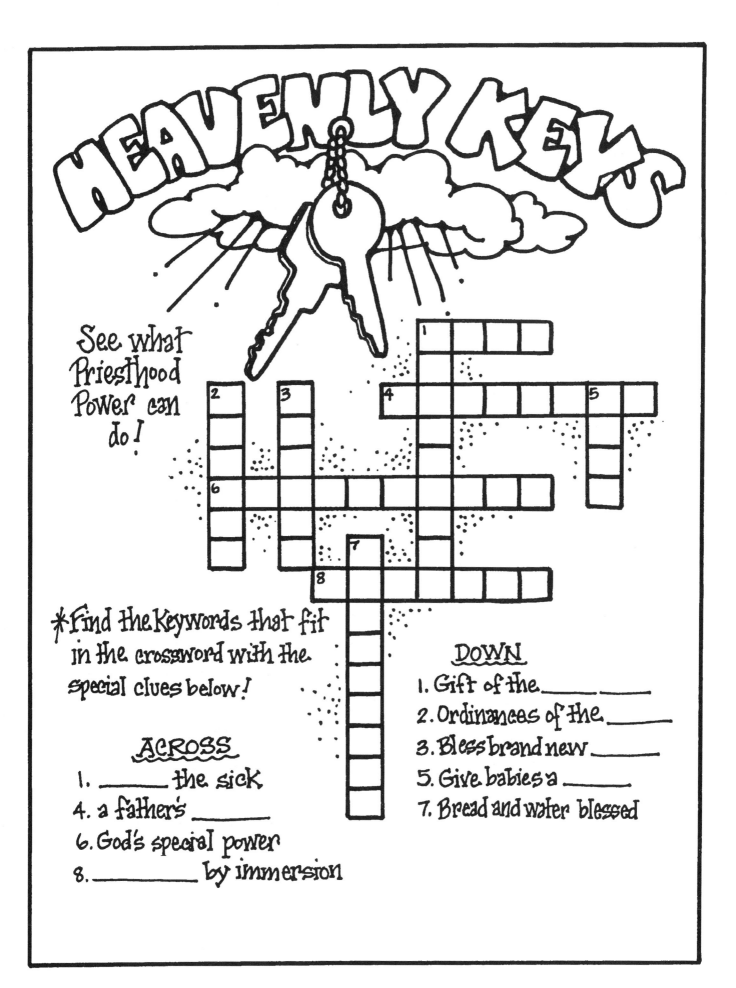

See what Priesthood Power can do!

*Find the Keywords that fit in the crossword with the special clues below!

ACROSS
1. _____ the sick
4. a father's _____
6. God's special power
8. _____ by immersion

DOWN
1. Gift of the _____
2. Ordinances of the _____
3. Bless brand new _____
5. Give babies a _____
7. Bread and water blessed

REPENTANCE: *I Will Repent and Grow Closer to the Savior*

BITE-SIZE MEMORIZE

Behold, he who has repented of his sins, the same is forgiven, and I, the Lord, remember them no more.
D&C 58:42

PREPARE AHEAD: Scripture Lesson, Bite-size Memorize Poster, Activity, and Thought Treat
OPENING SONG/PRAYER: "Repentance," page 98 in the Children's Songbook*
BITE-SIZE MEMORIZE: Present the D&C 58:42 poster (shown right) on page 97. Color poster and display to learn.
SCRIPTURE LESSON: Search and ponder scriptures below.

REPENTANCE: *I Will Repent and Grow Closer to the Savior*

Jesus suffered for the sins of everyone who repents. . . . . . .D&C 19:16
What is sin? . . . . James 4:17, 1 John 5:17
Jesus and Heavenly Father want us to grow close to them and return to
our heavenly home. . . . . Moses 6:57

WHAT IS REPENTANCE?
♥ REPENTANCE means you don't make excuses for your sin, you repent. . . . . Alma 42:29-30
♥ REPENTANCE means to say you are sorry for sin. . Psalms 38:18, D&C 58:43, 2 Corinthians 7:9-10
♥ REPENTANCE means to forgive yourself and others for "trespasses"—wrongdoing. Matthew 6:14-15
♥ REPENTANCE means to make peace (forgive). Ephesians 4:32, 3 Nephi 13:14-15, D&C 58:42; 64:9
♥ REPENTANCE means you are willing to keep the commandments of God. . . . . D&C 1:32
   WHO SHOULD REPENT? Everyone. .Ecclesiastes 7:20, 1 John 1:8
   WHY SHOULD WE REPENT?
♥ REPENTANCE and baptism are necessary for salvation. . . . . 2 Nephi 9:23, D&C 20:37; 42:28
♥ REPENTANCE brings forgiveness. . . . . .Isaiah 1:18, Mosiah 26:28-32
♥ REPENTANCE brings safety (repent or perish). . . . . . . .Matthew 9:10-13, Luke 13:3, Ezekiel 18:30
♥ REPENTANCE brings joy. . . . . Alma 36:10-28
♥ REPENTANCE shows you have the courage to Choose The Right. . . . . .Alma 53:20-21
♥ REPENTANCE shows you accept the sacrifice Jesus made so you can be forgiven. . . . . .Luke 23:34
♥ REPENTANCE helps you release burdens and return to God. . . . . .1 Nephi 15:33-35, D&C 61:2
   HOW SHOULD WE REPENT?
♥ REPENTANCE should be done daily (while in mortality). . . . . .2 Nephi 2:21, Alma 34:32
♥ REPENTANCE steps. . . . . Mosiah 4:10-12
♥ REPENTANCE means to make right the wrong you have done. . . . . Ezekiel 33:15-16

HOME-SPUN FUN ACTIVITIES: Select activities from the following pages to make learning fun.
CLOSING SONG/PRAYER: "Help Me Dear Father," page 99 in Children's Songbook*
THOUGHT TREAT: Smile Sandwich. Make miniature sandwiches and decorate with a cheese smile from a pressurized tube or can. Tell children that when we repent we become happy.
MORE LESSON IDEAS: IDEA #1—*Gospel Principles** Chapter 19 (pages 122-127)
IDEA #2—Primary lessons found in the *Primary** manuals (see LESSON IDEAS on pages 95-96)
IDEA #3—*Family Home Evening Resource Book** (pages 39-42)
IDEA #4—*Uniform System for Teaching the Gospel** missionary discussions #2 (pages 2-14, 15)
IDEA #5—*New Testament Stories** "Jesus Suffers in the Garden of Gethsemane," pages 111-114
IDEA #6—*Book of Mormon Reader** "Alma the Younger Repents," pages 56-59

REPENTANCE *Activities and Lesson Ideas*

REPENTANCE Heals
(repentance bandage breastplate)

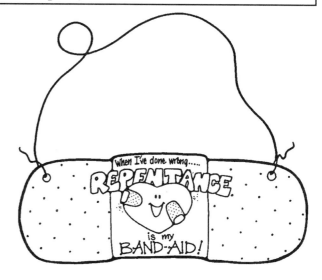

LESSON IDEAS: See lesson #10 in Primary 3-CTR B manual*.

YOU'LL NEED: Copy of bandage breastplate (page 98) on colored cardstock paper, and 25" piece of yarn or ribbon for each child, scissors, paper punch, and crayons. OPTION: Decorate each bandage breastplate with a small bandage.

AGES 3-7 ACTIVITY:
1. Color and cut out repentance bandage breastplate and glue-on stickers.
2. Punch a hole on each side.
3. Tie end of ribbon or string in left and right holes.
4. Hang around child's neck and over chest.
OPTION: Place a small bandage on breastplate to decorate.

THOUGHT TREAT: Bandage Gum. You'll find novelty gum in the candy section. As children open gum and chew, ask them to say, "When I've done wrong, repentance is my band-aid! I 'chew's to repent."

REPENTANCE: If I Can Say Hippopotamus, I Can Say I'm Sorry.
(hippo sack puppet)

LESSON IDEAS: See lesson #29 in Primary 1 manual*.

YOU'LL NEED: Copy hippo puppet (page 99) on brown or gray cardstock paper, small lunch sack for each child, glue, scissors, and crayons

AGES 3-7 ACTIVITY: Children can enjoy saying "I'm sorry" with their hippo sack puppet. With the sack, rehearse the word "hippopotamus." If they can say this big word, they can say "I'm sorry" when they do something wrong.
1. Color and cut out hippo face.
2. Glue hippo head on bottom of sack, and jaw in the middle of the sack. When fingers move sack flap up and down, hippo's mouth opens wide as child says "I'm sorry."

THOUGHT TREAT: Animal crackers or cookies (Look for the hippos!)

*Primary manuals are published by The Church of Jesus Christ of Latter-day Saints, Salt Lake City, Utah.

REPENTANCE *Activities and Lesson Ideas*

REPENTANCE: I Am Happy I Can Live in Heaven
(Alma the Younger's Road to Repentance maze)

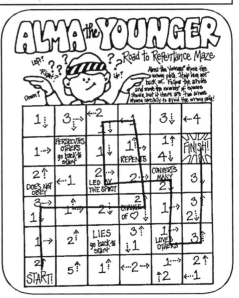

LESSON IDEAS: See lesson #14 in Primary 4 manual*.

YOU'LL NEED: Copy of repentance maze (page 100) on colored cardstock paper for each child, pencils, glue, and crayons

AGE 8-TEENS ACTIVITY: To remind children that repentance is necessary for earthly happiness and eternal life, get through this repentance maze. HOW TO GET THROUGH MAZE: Alma the Younger chose the wrong path. Help him get back on. Read the choice and choose for yourself the direction to go in order to repent and choose the righteous path.

THOUGHT TREAT: Repentance Iron Rod. Give children a candy bar that is straight and long to eat as you tell them the following: "If we repent and obey our Heavenly Father's commandments, we are holding on to the iron rod. This iron rod will guide us back to our Heavenly Father's presence. One way to hold to the iron rod is to read the scriptures. The iron rod is the word of God found in the scriptures and through the words of the prophet." Sing "The Iron Rod," page 274 in Hymns* songbook.

REPENTANCE: Jesus Made it Possible for Me to Repent
(REPENTANCE puzzle)

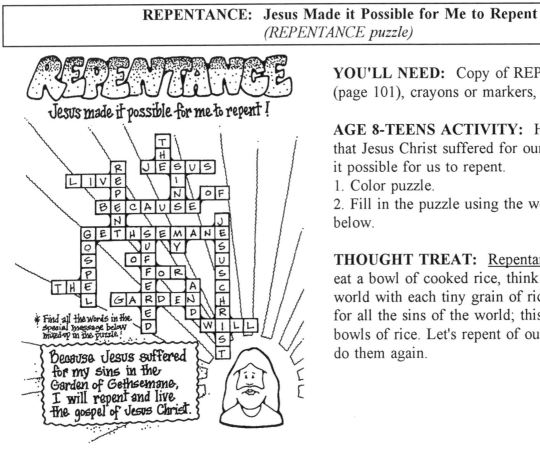

YOU'LL NEED: Copy of REPENTANCE puzzle (page 101), crayons or markers, and pencil

AGE 8-TEENS ACTIVITY: Help children know that Jesus Christ suffered for our sins, which makes it possible for us to repent.
1. Color puzzle.
2. Fill in the puzzle using the words in the statement below.

THOUGHT TREAT: Repentance Rice. As you eat a bowl of cooked rice, think about the sins of the world with each tiny grain of rice. Jesus suffered for all the sins of the world; this could be several bowls of rice. Let's repent of our sins and try not to do them again.

*Primary manual and Hymns songbook are published by The Church of Jesus Christ of Latter-day Saints, Salt Lake City, Utah.

Behold, he who has repented of his sins, the same is forgiven, and I, the Lord, remember them no more.

D&C 58:42

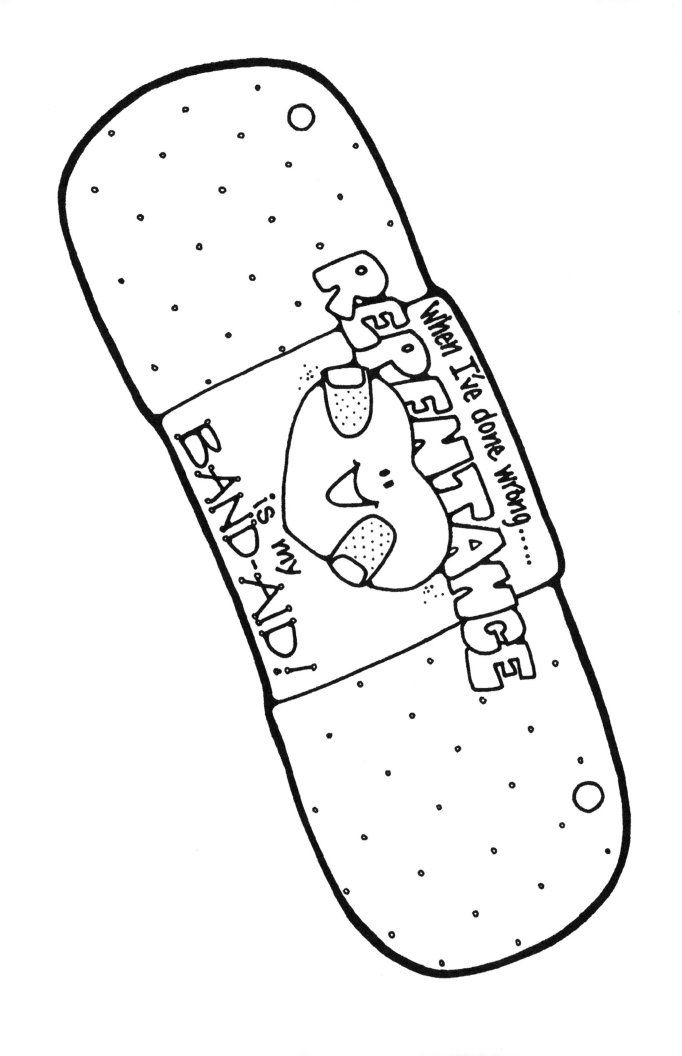

ALMA the YOUNGER

Road to Repentance Maze

Left? Right? Down? Up?

Alma the younger chose the wrong path. Help him get back on. Follow the arrows and move the number of spaces shown, but if there are two arrows choose carefully to avoid the wrong path!

1 ↓	3 ⋯→ ↓	←⋯2 1 ↓	←⋯1	3 ↓	←⋯4
1 ⋯→	PERSECUTES OTHERS go back to start	1 ↓	1 ↑⋯→ REPENTS	1 ↑ 4 ↓	FINISH!
2 ↑ DOES NOT OBEY	←⋯1	2 ⋯→ LED BY THE SPIRIT	2 ⋯→	CONVERTS MANY 2 ↓	3 ↓
3 ⋯→ 1 ↓	1 ↑⋯→	2 ↓	2 ↑ CHANGE OF ♡ ↓	1 ⋯→	3 ↑ 2 ↓
1 ⋯→	2 ↑	LIES go back to start	3 ↑ ↓1	1 ⋯→ LOVES OTHERS	3 ↑
2 ↑ START!	5 ↑	1 ↑	←⋯2⋯→	1 ⋯→ ↑2	2 ↑ ←⋯1

REPENTANCE

Jesus made it possible for me to repent !

* Find all the words in the special message below mixed-up in the puzzle!

Because Jesus suffered for my sins in the Garden of Gethsemane, I will repent and live the gospel of Jesus Christ.

SABBATH DAY: *I Will Keep the Sabbath Day Holy*

PREPARE AHEAD: Scripture Lesson, Bite-size Memorize Poster, Activity, and Thought Treat

OPENING SONG/PRAYER: "Saturday," page 196 in the Children's Songbook*

BITE-SIZE MEMORIZE: Present the D&C 59:10 poster (shown right) on page 105. Color poster and display to learn.

SCRIPTURE LESSON: Search and ponder scriptures below and on the following page.

SABBATH DAY: *I Will Keep the Sabbath Day Holy*

"Remember the Sabbath day to keep it holy." - Exodus 20:8
WORK DAYS 1-6 TO REST ON SABBATH . . . . Exodus 20:8-11,
. . . . D&C 109:8, Mosiah 13:16-19

SABBATH IS HOLY, MEANING *REST* (Hebrew) . . . . D&C 68:29, Exodus 20:8, Genesis 2:2-3
HOW WE CAN KEEP THE SABBATH DAY HOLY:
♥ Worship and partake of sacrament. . . . . .D&C 59:9-13, Mark 2:27
♥ Pray with our families. . . . . 3 Nephi 18:21
♥ Read the scriptures. . . . . 2 Nephi 4:15, Matthew 22:29, 3 Nephi 10:14, D&C 26:1, Mosiah 1:6-7
♥ Put our houses in order spiritually. . . . . .D&C 109:8, 16
♥ Learn about the gospel of Jesus Christ. . . . . D&C 109:7
♥ Search, ponder, and pray to learn truth. . . . . Moroni 10:4-5
♥ Counsel and plan with family. . . . . D&C 19:23-24; 109:8
♥ Fast for the welfare of others. . . . . Alma 6:6
♥ Pray and fast to receive the spirit to serve. . . . . .Alma 17:3, 9
♥ Read church magazines and books, and the prophet's words. . . . . D&C 21:4-7

BLESSINGS COME FROM KEEPING THE SABBATH DAY HOLY. . . . .Isaiah 58:13-14, Mark 2:27
. . . . D&C 59:15-19, Genesis 2:1-3

WHO SHOULD KEEP THE SABBATH DAY HOLY?
♥ SABBATH is for all to keep holy. . . . . Isaiah 56:1-8, D&C 68:29
♥ SABBATH observed by others. . . . . .Jarom 1:5, Jeremiah 17:19-27, Nephemiah 13:15-22

HOME-SPUN FUN ACTIVITIES: Select activities from the following pages to make learning fun.

CLOSING SONG/PRAYER: "Remember the Sabbath Day," page 155 in Children's Songbook*

THOUGHT TREAT: <u>Sabbath Soup</u>. Purchase or make soup with ABC—alphabet type noodles. As you sip your soup, find letters that start with commandments or words that remind you of the Sabbath.

MORE LESSON IDEAS: IDEA #1—*Gospel Principles** Chapter 24 (pages 159-163)
IDEA #2—Primary lessons found in the *Primary** manuals (see LESSON IDEAS, pages 103-104)
IDEA #3—*Family Home Evening Resource Book** (pages 218-219)
IDEA #4—*Old Testament Stories** "Jesus Makes the Earth," (pages 9-14——rested on 7th day)
IDEA #5—*Old Testament Stories** "The Ten Commandments," (pages 75-78——#4 keep Sabbath holy)

SABBATH DAY *Activities and Lesson Ideas*

SABBATH DAY: A Day to Remember
(Sabbath Day medallion)

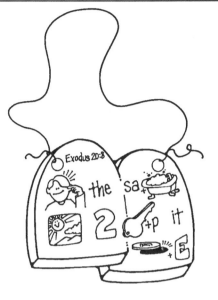

LESSON IDEAS: See lesson #37 in Primary 2-CTR A manual*.

YOU'LL NEED: Copy of medallion (page 106) on colored cardstock paper and 24" yarn or ribbon for each child, scissors, paper punch, and crayons

AGES 3-7 ACTIVITY: Create a picture message medallion to strengthen each child's desire to keep the Sabbath Day a holy day.
1. Color and cut out medallion.
2. Help children figure out message and memorize the scripture.
3. Punch holes at top left and right.
4. Tie a string at each end to hang around child's neck.
Show how child can hang medallion on the wall or door.

THOUGHT TREAT: Sabbath Sandwich. Make a sandwich, cut off crust and cut in fourths, then with processed cheese in a tube or can squirt an "S" on each for Sunday or Sabbath Day.

SUNDAY WORSHIP: I Want to Worship at Church
(Sunday block game)

LESSON IDEAS: See lesson #40 in Primary 3-CTR B manual*.

YOU'LL NEED: Copy of "I Want to Worship at Church" Sunday block (page 107) on colored cardstock paper for each child, scissors, glue, and crayons

AGES 3-7 ACTIVITY: Show ways to enjoy worshipping at church, one way to keep the Sabbath Day holy.
1. Color and cut out Sunday block game.
2. Fold game into a block.
3. Fold flaps inside block and glue.
TO PLAY THE SUNDAY BLOCK GAME:
1. Take turns rolling one block.
2. Each side of the die (block) shows a way that we can worship at church. For example, if "sacrament" lands face up, have the child tell how we can worship during the sacrament. For "listen," have child tell what we can learn as we listen. For "sing," have child give his favorite Primary song. For "pray," have child say what we can pray for.
3. When block lands on the girl and boy, ask a child what they like about going to church on Sunday.
4. When block lands on "I Want to Worship at Church," say, "I want to worship at church."

THOUGHT TREAT: Hard Tack Candy. As children suck on candy, they can think of how quiet we must be while we worship at church.

SABBATH DAY *Activities and Lesson Ideas*

SABBATH DAY: I Will Keep the Sabbath Day Holy
(Sabbath Day Decision Drama or Draw)

LESSON IDEAS: See lesson #41 in Primary 5 manual*.

YOU'LL NEED: Copy of jar label and wordstrips
(pages 108-109) on lightweight paper, scissors, and a jar with a lid

AGES 8-TEEN ACTIVITY: Help children learn the difference between right and wrong Sabbath Day activities. Cut out "Yes" and "No" wordstrips and place in a jar.

DECISION DRAMA OR DRAW: Children can play this by dividing into teams sitting across from the opposing team. Take turns drawing a wordstrip from a jar and reading it silently.

      OPTION #1 DRAMA: Act out the activity.

      OPTION #2 DRAW: Draw activity on the chalkboard.

The first team to guess the activity and vote "yes" (good Sabbath activity) or vote "no" (not a good Sabbath activity) wins a point for their team. Play, voting on all wordstrips or until time runs out.

THOUGHT TREAT: Sabbath Day Scripture Squiggles. Make cheese squiggles (wavy lines) on soda crackers or frosting squiggles (wavy lines) on graham crackers to remind children of a favorite Sabbath Day activity ... that of reading the scriptures.

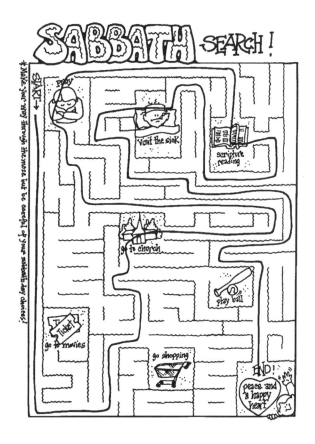

SABBATH DAY: Choose Sabbath Day Activities
("Sabbath Search" maze)

LESSON IDEAS: See lesson #14 in Primary 7 manual*.

YOU'LL NEED: Copy of "Sabbath Search" maze (page 110), crayons or markers, and pencil

AGES 8-TEEN ACTIVITY: Help children create and go through a "Sabbath Search" maze to find activities that are appropriate for Sunday. By doing these things, they honor Jesus and are rewarded with a happy heart.

1. Color and cut out "Sabbath Search" maze.

2. Draw with a pencil through the maze to get to the happy heart. Maze ends at wrong Sabbath day choices.

THOUGHT TREAT: Sunday Sundae. Create an ice cream sundae with ice cream and toppings. Talk about the sweet messages you receive when you attend church on Sunday or read the scriptures.

*Primary manuals are published by The Church of Jesus Christ of Latter-day Saints, Salt Lake City, Utah.

BITE-SIZE MEMORIZE

For verily this is a day appointed unto you to rest from your labors, and to pay thy devotions unto the Most High.

D&C 59:10

Sing

Pray

Listen

Sacrament

I want to
worship
at church.

PATTERN: *SABBATH DAY (Decision Drama or Draw)*

Ride your bike	NO	Watch a church video	YES
Shop for groceries	NO	Read church magazines	YES
Walk the dog	YES	Put on a scripture play	YES
Write letters	YES	Mop the floor	NO
Visit the sick	YES	Read brother or sister a story	YES
Go skiing	NO	Listen to spiritual music	YES
Pay your tithing	YES	Help prepare a simple meal	YES
Go to church	YES	Read a book the prophet wrote	YES
Visit with family	YES	Play quiet games with the family	YES
Read the scriptures	YES	Have family prayer	YES
Have family home evening	YES	Color a picture	YES
Do the dishes	YES	Play ball	NO
Clean the house	NO	Write in your journal	YES
Mow the lawn	NO	Take notes in church	YES
Clean the garage	NO	Listen to your teacher	YES
Wash the car	NO	Participate in Primary	YES
Suntan	NO	Sit reverently in church	YES
Go swimming	NO	Visit grandparents	YES
Eat out at a restaurant	NO	Invite a friend to church	YES
Make a card for someone	YES	Do a kind deed	YES
Make your bed	YES	Talk to your brother or sister	YES
Play the piano	YES	Go for a short walk	YES
Sing	YES	Take a nap	YES
Go fishing	NO	Bake cookies	NO
Play sports	NO	Help set the table	YES
Do homework	NO	Iron clothes	NO
Wash your hair	YES	Shine shoes	NO

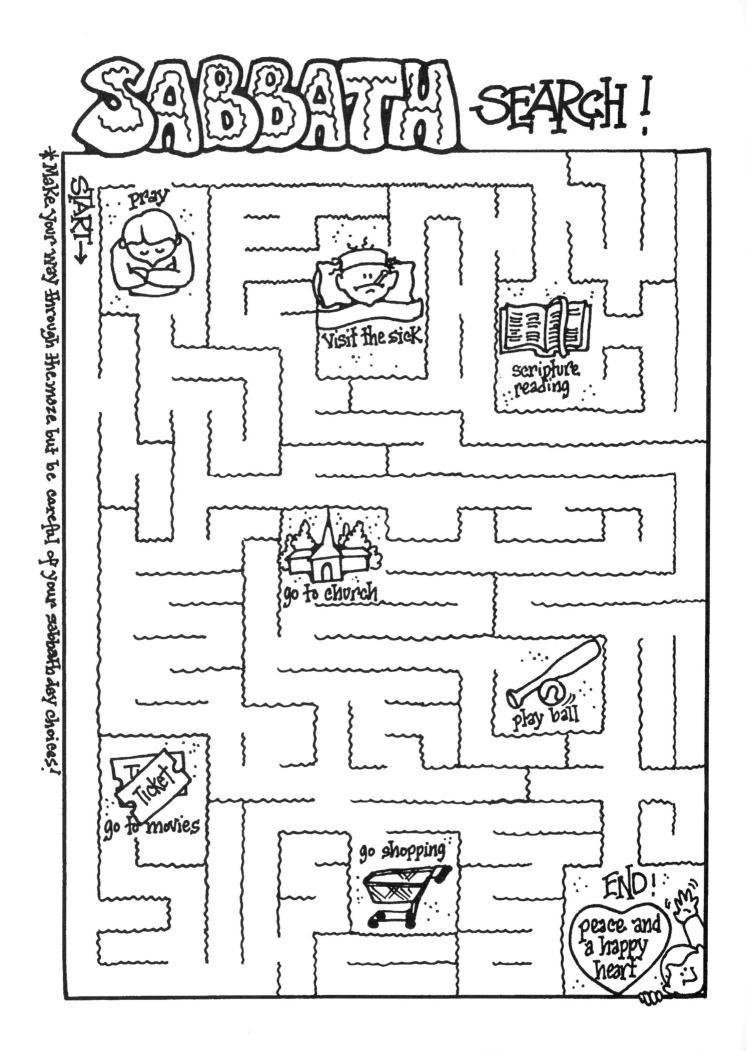

SACRAMENT: *I Will Keep the Commandments and Remember Jesus*

PREPARE AHEAD: Scripture Lesson, Bite-size Memorize Poster, Activity, and Thought Treat

OPENING SONG/PRAYER: "Before I Take the Sacrament," page 73 in the Children's Songbook*

BITE-SIZE MEMORIZE: Present the John 15:13 poster (shown right) on page 114. Color poster and display to learn.

SCRIPTURE LESSON: Search and ponder scriptures below.

> *SACRAMENT: I Will Keep the Commandments and Remember Jesus*

- ♥ SACRAMENT is a priesthood ordinance. . . . . 3 Nephi 18:5
- ♥ SACRAMENT was brought to the Apostles by Jesus Christ before his crucifixion. He wanted them to always remember him and to keep his commandments.
- ♥ SACRAMENT was brought to the Nephites by Jesus after his resurrection. . . . . 3 Nephi 18:1-12
- ♥ SACRAMENT is offered to us each Sunday in sacrament meeting. . . . . D&C 20:75
- ♥ SACRAMENT allows us to remember baptismal promises. . . . . .D&C 20:37, Mosiah 18:6-10
- ♥ SACRAMENT helps us to think of Jesus and find peace. .D&C 19:23-24
- ♥ SACRAMENT helps us remember Jesus to have his spirit to be with us. . . . . .3 Nephi 18:7, 11
- ♥ SACRAMENT bread represents Jesus' body *"which I give a ransom for you."* . . . .
  . . . . Matthew 26:26 (see JST footnote)
- ♥ SACRAMENT water represents Jesus' blood *"which is shed for many as shall believe on my name, for the remission of their sins."* . . . . Matthew 26:24-25 (JST),
  . . . . Mark 14:22-24, Luke 22:15-20, D&C 20:77
- ♥ SACRAMENT is to remember Jesus Christ, who took our sins upon him. . . . . .Hebrews 9:28; 13:12,
  . . . . Mosiah 3:5-8
- ♥ SACRAMENT shows Jesus is the "gate" through which we enter heaven. . . .John 14:6, 2 Nephi 9:41
- ♥ SACRAMENT reminds us that Jesus suffered and gave his life for us that we might have a remission of our sins. . . . . John 19:16-20, Mosiah 4:1-2, Alma 42:14-15, 2 Nephi 2:6-9

HOME-SPUN FUN ACTIVITIES: Select activities from the following pages to make learning fun.

CLOSING SONG/PRAYER: "To Think About Jesus," page 71 in Children's Songbook*

THOUGHT TREAT: Unleavened Bread. Share with children some flat (pita) bread or fry bread, the type of bread Jesus may have served during the first sacrament (yeast free). Break some off and let the children taste it and think of the first sacrament.

MORE LESSON IDEAS: IDEA #1—*Gospel Principles** Chapter 23 (pages 151-156)
IDEA #2—Primary lessons found in the *Primary** manuals (see LESSON IDEAS, pages 112-113)
IDEA #3—*Family Home Evening Resource Book** (pages 56-63)
IDEA #4—*New Testament Stories** "The First Sacrament," pages 108-110
IDEA #5—*New Testament Stories** "Jesus Is Crucified," pages 115-120
IDEA #6—*Book of Mormon Reader** "Jesus Christ Comes to America," page 93—3 Nephi 18:1-10

*Songbook and suggested lesson materials are published by The Church of Jesus Christ of Latter-day Saints, Salt Lake City, Utah.

SACRAMENT *Activities and Lesson Ideas*

SACRAMENT: Remembering Jesus
(Last Supper shadow box)

LESSON IDEAS: See lesson #32 in Primary 3-CTR B manual*.

YOU'LL NEED: Copy of shadow box, Jesus and his apostles (page 115) on colored cardstock paper for each child, scissors, glue or tape, and crayons

AGES 3-7 ACTIVITY: Create a Last Supper shadow box and review what happened at the Last Supper (Matthew 26:17-30). This will help the children remember Jesus and the first sacrament. Jesus asked the apostles to take the sacrament to remember him. Each week in sacrament meeting, we take the sacrament to show Heavenly Father that we remember Jesus.

AGES 8-TEENS: Create shadow box and tell about Jesus giving the sacrament to the Nephites (3 Nephi 18:1-11; 20:1-9). Also, talk about the Last Supper (detailed above).

TO MAKE SHADOW BOX: (1) Color and cut out shadow box and figures. (2) Fold figure tabs. (3) Glue figure tabs in place on box.

SACRAMENT: Reminds Us of Our Promises
(sacrament and baptism covenant flip-card)

LESSON IDEAS: See lesson #33 in Primary 3-CTR B manual*.

YOU'LL NEED: Copy of two-sided covenant flip-card and glue-on sticker patterns (page 116) on colored cardstock paper, and a wooden craft stick for each child, scissors, glue, and crayons

AGES 3-7 ACTIVITY: Create a two-sided flip-card to show on one side: "As I take the sacrament I will remember my baptism promises." On the other side: "I promise to: Always remember Jesus, and obey the commandments."

TO MAKE FLIP CARD: (1) Color and cut out flip card and glue-on stickers. (2) Fold card in half. (3) Place a wooden craft stick in the center of card and glue the top half of the stick on card half way up. (4) Glue card back-to-back. (5) Glue baptism and sacrament stickers in place.

THOUGHT TREAT: Smile Face Sandwich. Make a tuna or lunch meat sandwich and place a piece of cheese with a smile face on top. Wrap sandwich or place in a plastic bag. How to Make Smile Face Cheese: Cut a square piece of cheese with a round cookie cutter or jar lid. Carve out diamond shaped eyes and nose, and round mouth. NOTE: Tell children that being baptized and taking the sacrament makes you happy because you are choosing the right, and doing what Jesus did.

SACRAMENT *Activities and Lesson Ideas*

SACRAMENT: I Like to Remember Jesus
(sacrament manners match game)

LESSON IDEAS: See lesson #40 in Primary 1 manual*.

YOU'LL NEED: Copy of match game cards
(page 117) on colored cardstock paper for each child,
scissors, and crayons

AGES 3-7 ACTIVITY: Assemble a match game for each
child and place in an envelope or zip-close plastic sandwich
bag to remind them of how they should act during the
sacrament.
COLOR AND CUT OUT CARD SETS.
TO PLAY: Turn cards face down. Take turns turning two
cards over to try and make a match. If cards match, keep
matching cards. If cards don't match, turn cards back over
and next player tries to make a match.

AGES 8-TEENS ACTIVITY: Scramble, race to find
scriptures to match cards and read aloud. Divide into teams
with one set of cards each. Write scripture references on the
back of cards. After 15 minutes, compare how many
scriptures are found that match the picture/subject.

SACRAMENT: I Will Remember Jesus
(sacrament symbols two-sided puzzle)

LESSON IDEAS: See lesson #36 in Primary 4 manual*.

YOU'LL NEED: Copy of two-sided puzzle (page 118) on
colored cardstock paper, and an envelope or plastic zip-close bag
for each child, scissors, glue, and crayons

AGES 8-TEENS ACTIVITY: Create a sacrament reminder
two-sided puzzle to help children always remember Jesus Christ
and to strive to have his spirit to be with them.
TWO-SIDED PUZZLE: Side 1 of puzzle reminds child of the
body (3 Nephi 18:7) and side 2 of the blood shed for them
(3 Nephi 18:11). Help the children do side 1 puzzle matching the
scripture, then side two. Tell them about Jesus bringing the
sacrament to the Nephites.

1. Color and cut out edge of puzzle.
2. Fold puzzle in half on dividing line back-to-back.
3. Glue puzzle together (spreading glue over the entire piece, not
just the edges).
4. Trim edges. Cut puzzle shapes out as shown on one side.
5. Place puzzle in an envelope or plastic bag for each child.

*Primary manuals are published by The Church of Jesus Christ of Latter-day Saints, Salt Lake City, Utah.

I will remember Jesus.

The Last Supper

The Sacrament

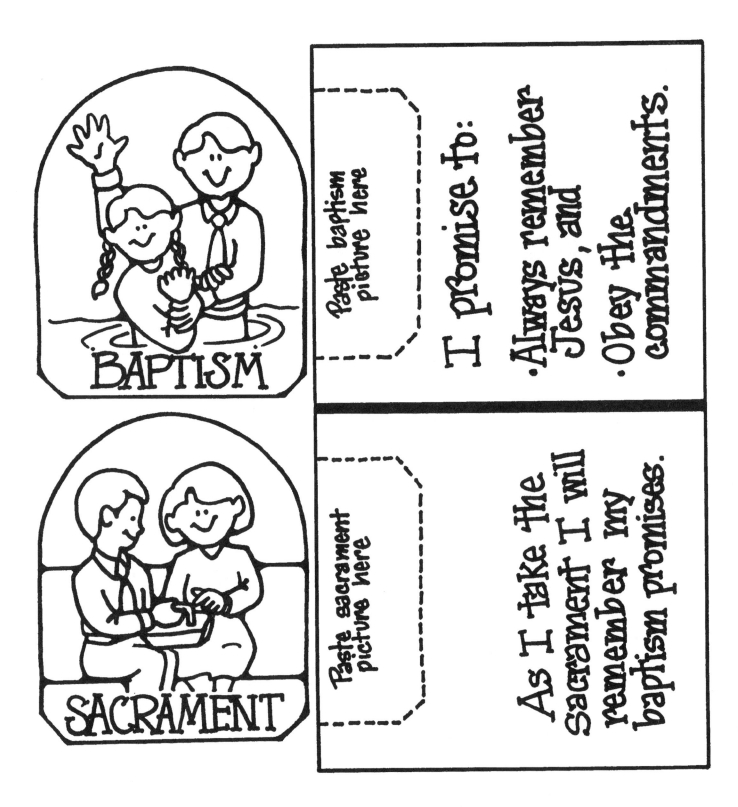

BAPTISM

SACRAMENT

Paste baptism picture here

I promise to:
- Always remember Jesus, and
- Obey the commandments.

Paste sacrament picture here

As I take the sacrament I will remember my baptism promises.

PATTERN: *SACRAMENT (manners match game)*

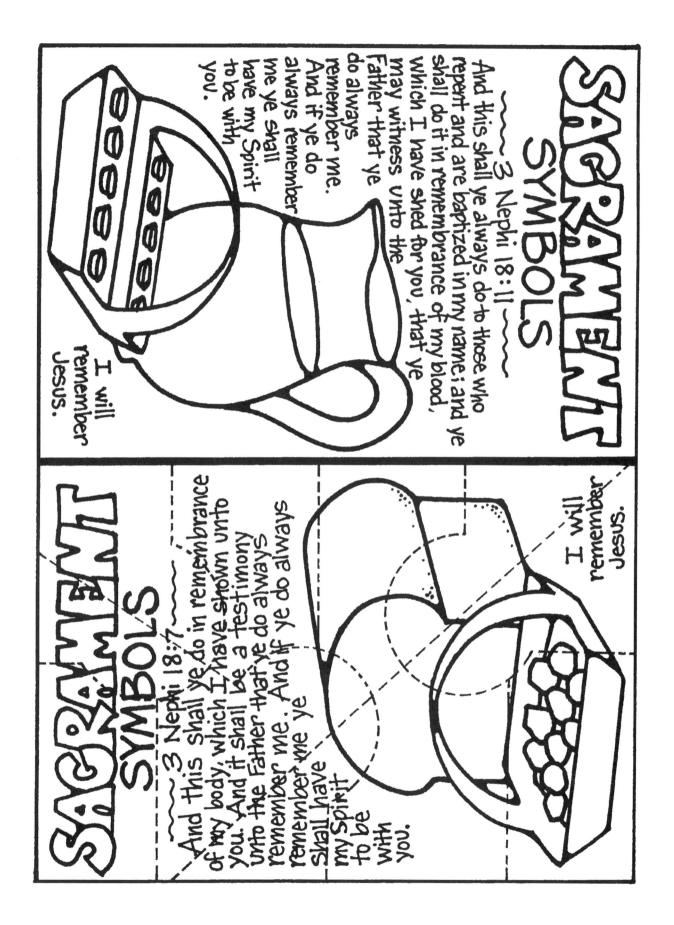

SACRAMENT
SYMBOLS

~~ 3 Nephi 18:11 ~~

And this shall ye always do to those who repent and are baptized in my name; and ye shall do it in remembrance of my blood, which I have shed for you, that ye may witness unto the Father that ye do always remember me. And if ye do always remember me, ye shall have my Spirit to be with you.

I will remember Jesus.

SACRAMENT
SYMBOLS

~~ 3 Nephi 18:7 ~~

And this shall ye do in remembrance of my body, which I have shown unto you. And it shall be a testimony unto the Father that ye do always remember me. And if ye do always remember me ye shall have my Spirit to be with you.

I will remember Jesus.

TESTIMONY: *I Will Strengthen My Testimony of the Church of Jesus Christ*

PREPARE AHEAD: Scripture Lesson, Bite-size Memorize Poster, Activity, and Thought Treat

OPENING SONG/PRAYER: "Search, Ponder, and Pray," page 109 in the Children's Songbook*

BITE-SIZE MEMORIZE: Present the D&C 62:3 poster (shown right) on page 122. Color poster and display to learn.

SCRIPTURE LESSON: Search and ponder scriptures below.

> *TESTIMONY: I Will Strengthen My Testimony of the Church of Jesus Christ*

BITE-SIZE MEMORIZE

D&C 62:3

Nevertheless, ye are blessed, for the testimony which ye have borne is recorded in heaven for the angels to look upon, and they rejoice over you, and your sins are forgiven you.

Testimony is a belief in the Savior Jesus Christ, and that the gospel of Jesus Christ is true. Testimony is the light that guides us to eternal life. . . .Alma 7:16, 2 Nephi 33:4

By living the principles of the gospel of Jesus Christ, we can become like him. The more we live these principles, the stronger our testimony becomes (seeds of faith). . . . . Alma 32:28

<u>These are things we can testify to others when we BEAR OUR TESTIMONY.</u>

♥ I know that I am a child of God. . . . . .Psalm 82:6, Mosiah 4:15, D&C 14:7
♥ The Church of Jesus Christ of Latter-day Saints is true (light to world). . . . . D&C 115:4-5
♥ The Book of Mormon is true. . . . . .Mosiah 1:6, 2 Nephi 4:15
♥ Jesus Christ lives and loves me. . .Nephi 11:10-14, Luke 24:36-43, 3 Nephi 11:8-10, J.S. History 1:17
♥ I can gain my testimony from Heavenly Father and Jesus Christ. . . . . . .Moroni 10:5, D&C 18:34-36
♥ The Holy Ghost tells me that these things are true. . . . . . 1 Nephi 10:19, Alma 5:45-47, Moroni 10:5
♥ I know that the prophet lives and guides us in these latter-days. . . . . . . Joseph Smith—History 1:1-20

HOW TO GAIN A TESTIMONY: Moroni gave us the Book of Mormon Promise. . . . Moroni 10:4-5
(1) Desire a testimony—1 Nephi 2:16 (2) Study—John 8:32, Mosiah 1:7 (3) Keep the commandments —Mosiah 2:41, Alma 32:41 (4) Let the seed of faith grow daily—Alma 32:28-43 (5) Seek truth —Moroni 10:4 (6) Learn from the testimony of others—1 Samuel 3, Mormon 1:13-15, 1 Nephi 2:16-24 (7) Repent and receive forgiveness—Mosiah 4:3 (8) Live gospel principles—Ether 12:6 (9) Ask Heavenly Father—D&C 42:51 (9) Be a missionary—Alma 32:23, Romans 1:16, D&C 4:2-3; 133:8, 37

HOME-SPUN FUN ACTIVITIES: Select activities from the following pages to make learning fun.

CLOSING SONG/PRAYER: "The Church of Jesus Christ," page 77 in Children's Songbook*

THOUGHT TREAT: <u>Testimony Ties.</u> Share long strings of licorice, each one tied in a knot. Tell children: This knot is like our testimony of the scriptures. It helps us hold tight to the iron rod (the word of God). If we hold tight to the iron rod, we can walk the straight and narrow path that leads us to eternal life.

MORE LESSON IDEAS: IDEA #1—*Gospel Principles* Chapters 7-10 (pages 36-52)
IDEA #2—Primary lessons found in the *Primary* manuals (see LESSON IDEAS on pages 120-121)
IDEA #3—*Family Home Evening Resource Book* (pages 69-73, 115)
IDEA #4—*Uniform System for Teaching the Gospel* missionary discussions #1 (pages 1-14 - 1-20)
IDEA #5—*Book of Mormon Reader* "Mormon and Moroni/Book of Mormon Promise," pages 97-102
IDEA #6—*Book of Mormon Reader* "How We Got the Book of Mormon," pages 6-8

*Songbook and suggested lesson materials are published by The Church of Jesus Christ of Latter-day Saints, Salt Lake City, Utah.

TESTIMONY *Activities and Lesson Ideas*

TESTIMONY: I Will Bear My Testimony
(bear slide show/doorknob hanger)

LESSON IDEAS: See lesson #9 in Primary 5 manual*.

YOU'LL NEED: Copy of testimony bear slide show (pages 123-124) on colored cardstock paper for each child, scissors, glue, and crayons

AGES 3-7 ACTIVITY: Children can learn ways to be a witness of the Book of Mormon and its teachings. They can learn how to bear their testimony of the gospel of Jesus Christ. (1) Color and cut out bear, bow, and doorknob hanger (slide show). (2) Boys glue bow tie on bear and girls glue bow on head. (3) Glue part A and B together where shown. (4) Cut a slit in the top and bottom of square of bear's tummy. (5) Slide doorknob hanger (slide show wordstrips) down into bear to pull up and down. (6) Fold bottom flap of wordstrip to prevent slipping. (7) Children can hang this on their door.

THOUGHT TREAT: Testimony Bear Treats. Make a bear using a bear mold and Rice Krispies® recipe (on box of Kellogg's® cereal). Or, make bear using bread dough and bake. Or, give cinnamon candy bears to children. Ask children to bear their testimony, and then eat the bear.

TESTIMONY: I Can "Bear" My Testimony
(find the secret message)

LESSON IDEAS: See lesson #37 in Primary 7 manual*.

YOU'LL NEED: Copy of poster (page 125), pencil, and crayons for each child.

AGES 8-11 ACTIVITY: Create a poster with testimonies. Parents, don't let children know the secret message. Let them discover it on their own. This way children will know what to say when they bear their testimony. (1) Color poster. (2) Help children underline key words in different colors to find the secret message: "I KNOW THE GOSPEL OF JESUS CHRIST IS TRUE!" (3) Write secret message below.

THOUGHT TREAT: Testimony Tart. Serve tarts with berry filling and say, "A testimony is berry (very) sweet, just like this tart."

*Primary manuals are published by The Church of Jesus Christ of Latter-day Saints, Salt Lake City, Utah.

TESTIMONY *Activities and Lesson Ideas*

TESTIMONY: Study and Prayer Strengthen My Testimony
(TESTIMONY word race)

LESSON IDEAS: See lesson #46 in Primary 5 manual*.

YOU'LL NEED: Copy of TESTIMONY word design chart (page 126) on colored cardstock paper for each child, pencils, and crayons

AGES 8-TEENS ACTIVITY: Race to find words that stem from the word TESTIMONY. (1) Divide family into two teams with their TESTIMONY word design chart in front of them. (2) With pencil in hand and two teams with chairs back to back, begin. (3) Use the letters in TESTIMONY to inspire other words that connect. Words can be written in any direction—left, right, up, down, or diagonal. (4) Once a word is written, other words can stem off the words written. All words must be words that are part of the gospel of Jesus Christ, words that help strengthen testimony. (5) Children can earn <u>10</u> points for every word that stems from the word TESTIMONY. (6) Children can earn <u>1</u> point for all words written after the first word that stems from the word TESTIMONY. See chart on this page if you run out of ideas.

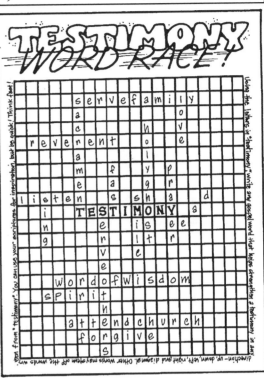

THOUGHT TREAT: <u>TESTIMONY Treats</u>. Any food that begins with the letters in the word TESTIMONY, i.e.: <u>t</u>affy, <u>e</u>gg, <u>s</u>alt, <u>t</u>oast, <u>i</u>cing or <u>i</u>ce cube, <u>m</u>ustard, <u>o</u>nion or <u>o</u>range, <u>n</u>ut or <u>n</u>oodle, <u>y</u>east, <u>y</u>ogurt, or <u>y</u>am. <u>Activity #1</u>: Place food items on a tray for children to see to play the memory game. Children can look at tray for 60 seconds (still divided into teams). <u>Activity #2</u>: Have children write the word TESTIMONY by placing treats in order, i.e., <u>t</u>oast first and <u>e</u>ggplant second. Be sure to share a treat with children, i.e., <u>t</u>affy, a dyed hard boiled <u>e</u>gg (with letter "T" written on shell), or a small container of <u>y</u>ogurt or <u>y</u>ogurt-covered raisins or peanuts.

TESTIMONY: I Will Strengthen My Testimony of Jesus Christ
(What Would Jesus Do? choice situations sack)

LESSON IDEAS: See lesson #8 in Primary 4 manual*.

YOU'LL NEED: Copy of choice situations and bag label (page 127) on colored cardstock paper, a zip-close plastic sandwich bag or small lunch sack, and peppermint candies (to place in bag) for each child, scissors, glue, pencils, and crayons

AGES 8-TEENS ACTIVITY: Help children make choices in advance to give them power to withstand evil influences. Ask them to choose what Jesus would do when temptation comes.
1. Color and cut out What Would Jesus Do? bag label to place inside a plastic bag or glue-mount on a paper bag.
2. Color and cut out choice situation cards and place inside bag.

THOUGHT TREAT: <u>Starlight Mints</u>. Place 8 mints in each child's bag. Children can choose a situation from the bag while they eat their mint and think what Jesus would do in that situation.

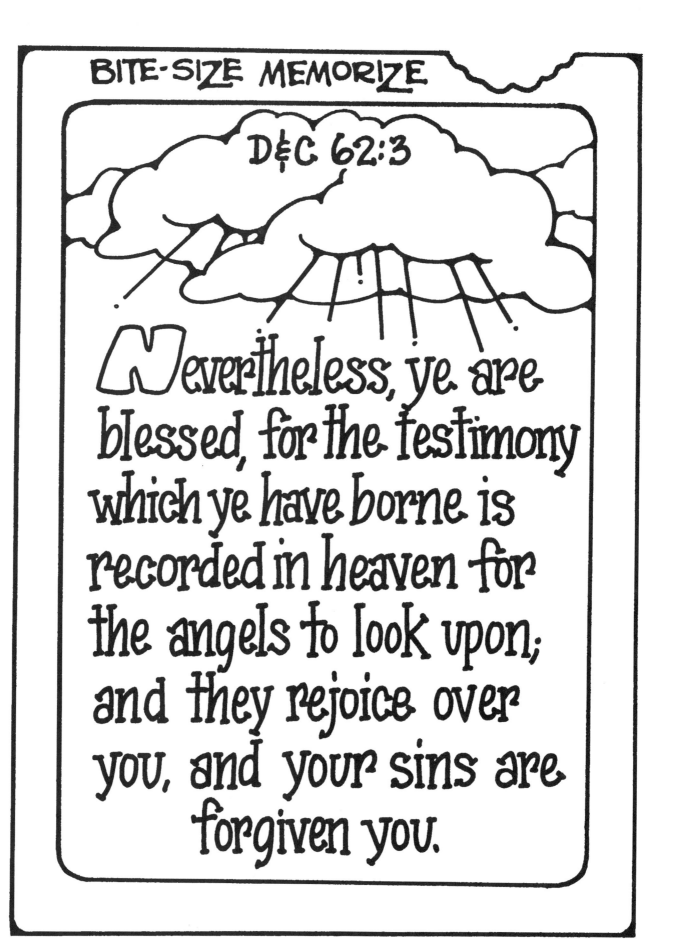

PATTERN: *TESTIMONY (slide show)*

*Bow can be a bowtie for the boys and a hair bow for the girls!

I will "bear" my testimony of truth.

Part A

Part B

Glue to part A

Joseph Smith translated the Book of Mormon through God's power.

The True Priesthood was restored.

We have a living Prophet today.

Jesus Christ lives and loves me.

The Holy Ghost speaks truth to my heart.

The Book of Mormon is true.

Joseph Smith is God's chosen prophet.

Fold back

I can BEAR my testimony!

I know the Book of Mormon is the Word of God.

Heavenly Father sent me to earth for a special purpose. He is the father of my spirit.

Jesus Christ is Heavenly Father's son. He came to earth to save us from sin.

Joseph Smith is God's chosen prophet. He restored the gospel of Jesus Christ in the latter days.

The church of Jesus Christ is the only true church.

We are led by apostles and prophets, just as in the days of old.

My Heavenly Father lives and answers my prayers.

*Using the words in the message below fill in the blanks.

I know the gospel of Jesus Christ is true!

TESTIMONY WORD RACE!

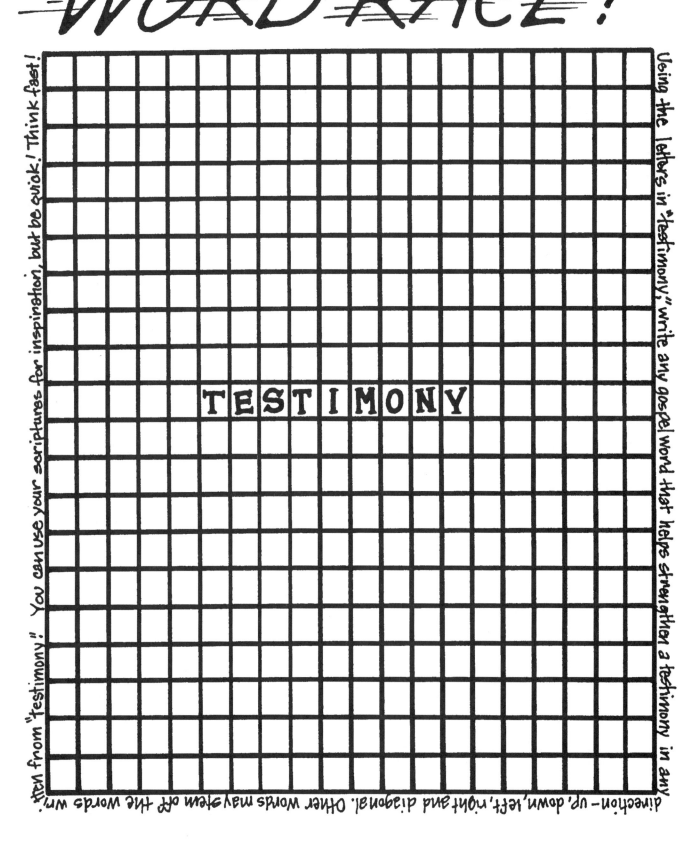

TESTIMONY

Using the letters in "testimony," write any gospel word that helps strengthen a testimony in any direction—up, down, left, right and diagonal. Other words may stem off the words written from "testimony." You can use your scriptures for inspiration, but be quick! Think fast!

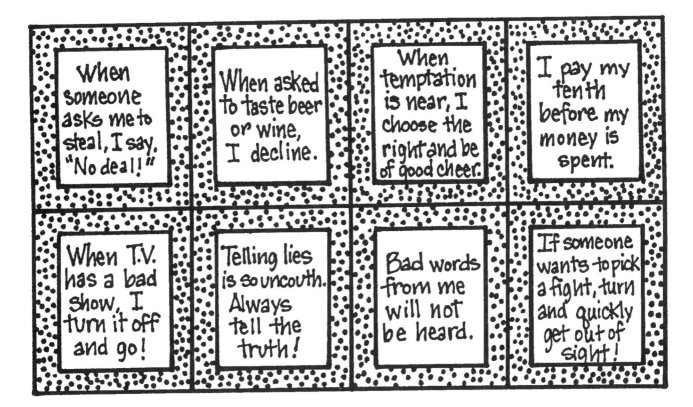

When someone asks me to steal, I say, "No deal!"

When asked to taste beer or wine, I decline.

When temptation is near, I choose the right and be of good cheer.

I pay my tenth before my money is spent.

When T.V. has a bad show, I turn it off and go!

Telling lies is so uncouth. Always tell the truth!

Bad words from me will not be heard.

If someone wants to pick a fight, turn and quickly get out of sight!

My testimony of Jesus Christ helps me make right choices. "Jesus mint" for me to be happy. So I must follow him.

What would Jesus do?

TITHING: *I Will Build Up the Kingdom of God*

PREPARE AHEAD: Scripture Lesson, Bite-size Memorize Poster, Activity, and Thought Treat

OPENING SONG/PRAYER: "I Want to Give the Lord My Tenth," page 150 in the Children's Songbook*

BITE-SIZE MEMORIZE: Present the Malachi 3:10 poster (shown right) on page 131. Color poster and display to learn.

SCRIPTURE LESSON: Search and ponder scriptures below.

BITE-SIZE MEMORIZE

Bring ye all the tithes into the store-🏠, that there may be 🍕 in mine house, and prove me now herewith, saith the Lord of hosts, if 👁 will not open you the 🪟s of ☁ and pour you out a blessing, that there shall not be room enough to receive it. Malachi 3:10

TITHING: *I Will Build Up the Kingdom of God*

Show the tithing bills (page 136) as you talk about points #1-3):

#1 I AM HAPPY TO HELP BY PAYING TITHING. . . . . 2 Corinthians 9:6-7
  ○ The Prophet Joseph Smith was given the law of tithing. . . . . D&C 119:3-6
  ○ Seek first the kingdom of God. . . . . Matthew 6:33
  ○ Give the Lord a portion of our increase. . . . . .Proverbs 3:9
  ○ Impart of your substance to build up the kingdom of God. . . . . Mosiah 18:27-28

#2 HEAVENLY FATHER WILL BLESS US WHEN WE PAY TITHING:
  ○ Windows of heaven open and blessings come. . . . . 3 Nephi 24:8-10, Malachi 3:10-12
  ○ Tithing shows we are willing to sacrifice (we will not be burned). . . . . .D&C 64:23; 85:3
  ○ Heavenly Father will take care of our needs. . . . . .3 Nephi 13:32-33, Matthew 6:32-33

#3 TITHING HELPS BUILD TEMPLES AND MEETINGHOUSES, SUSTAINS MISSIONARY
    WORK, SUPPORTS FAMILY HISTORY AND TEMPLE WORK. . . . . D&C 97:10-12

♥ TITHING PAID BY OTHERS: . . . . . . .Alma 13:15, Genesis 28:20-22, Nephemiah 10:37-38; 13:12,
. . . . 2 Chronicles 31:5-6, 12, Leviticus 27:30-32, 34, Mark 12:41-44, Hebrews 7:1-2
♥ PAY TITHING, EVEN THOUGH YOU HAVE LITTLE TO GIVE. . . . .Luke 21:1-4 (widow's mite)
♥ PAY TITHING TO BE HONEST WITH GOD. . . . . .Malachi 3:8-12
♥ PAY A FULL TITHING TO SHOW SERVICE TO GOD. . . . . 3 Nephi 13:24, Matthew 6:24
♥ PAY TITHING TO BUILD HEAVENLY TREASURES. . . . . Jacob 2:18-19, 3 Nephi 13:19-21,
. . . . Matthew 6:19-21
♥ HOW LONG DO WE PAY TITHING? . . . . .D&C 119:4

HOME-SPUN FUN ACTIVITIES: Select activities from the following pages to make learning fun.

CLOSING SONG/PRAYER: "I'm Glad to Pay a Tithing," page 150 in Children's Songbook*

THOUGHT TREAT: <u>Money Candies</u>. Purchase gold foil-wrapped chocolates in money shapes, or round flat candies in dime shapes (serve 10 each). Learn to count out 10% as you eat 9 out of the 10.

MORE LESSON IDEAS: IDEA #1—*Gospel Principles** Chapter 32 (pages 207-210)
IDEA #2—Primary lessons found in the *Primary** manuals (see LESSON IDEAS, pages 129-130)
IDEA #3—*Family Home Evening Resource Book** (pages 227-228)
IDEA #4—*Uniform System for Teaching the Gospel** missionary discussions #5 (pages 5-14, 15)
IDEA #5—*New Testament Stories** "The Widow's Mite," pages 94-95, "The Rich Young Man,"
page 92-93 (explain we are not asked to give all our riches, just 1/10th of our earnings to the Lord)

TITHING *Activities and Lesson Ideas*

TITHING: I Can Pay Tithing
(tithing purse with coins)

YOU'LL NEED: Copy of tithing purse and coins (pages 132-133) on colored cardstock paper for each child, scissors, crayons, and glue

AGES 3-7 ACTIVITY: Create a tithing purse for each child to help them practice counting coins. As they learn to hold back one coin out of ten to give to the bishop, they will be able to pay a real tithing when money is earned.
1. Color and cut out tithing purse.
2. Fold purse in half.
3. Glue together on sides and bottom, leaving top open.
4. Punch two holes at the top sides.
5. Tie yarn or ribbon through the holes at each end.
6. Cut out coins and place in purse.

THOUGHT TREAT: Ten Tithing Mints. Help children take out one mint to share. Tell children that Heavenly Father "mint" for us to share. We share as we pay our tithing.

TITHING: I Can Show Love As I Share
(tithing envelope)

LESSON IDEAS: See lesson #33 in Primary 2-CTR A manual*.

YOU'LL NEED: Copy of "My Tithing" envelope (page 134) and tithing receipt from bishop's office (optional) for each child, scissors, glue, and crayons

AGES 5-9 ACTIVITY: Create a tithing storage envelope for each child to store ready-to-pay tithing money and receipt forms. Explain that as we pay our tithing, we show love for Heavenly Father and Jesus. Help child fill out a sample tithing envelope, to put the tithing amount in later.
1. Color and cut out envelope.
2. Fold edges and glue like an envelope, leaving top flap free to open and close.

THOUGHT TREAT: Ten Bite-size Cookies. Help children give one to the bishop, explaining to the bishop of your ward that you are helping the children share 1/10th.

TITHING *Activities and Lesson Ideas*

TITHING: I Will Pay a Full Tithing to Build Up the Kingdom of God
(origami tithing purse/wallet)

LESSON IDEAS: See lesson #45 in Primary 5 manual*.

YOU'LL NEED: Copy of origami tithing purse/wallet (page 135) on colored cardstock paper for each child, scissors, and crayons

AGES 8-TEENS ACTIVITY: Fold a tithing purse/wallet to hold tithing donations until child has the opportunity to pay. This purse/wallet can be placed in their scriptures for safekeeping. Remind children that each time they open this envelope to put money in to keep for tithing or take the money out to pay tithing, they receive a blessing from heaven. (1) Color and cut out purse/wallet pattern. (2) Follow steps #A-G to fold purse/wallet.

THOUGHT TREATS:

OPTION #1: 1/10th Cupcake. Bake a cupcake for each child and one for the bishop. Give each child 10 M&M pieces of candy. Each child places one candy on the bishop's cupcake and nine on their cupcake. Deliver cupcake with donations to the bishop.

OPTION #2: Tithing Storehouse Cake. Bake and frost a cake. With different colored frosting tubes, decorate cake with a tithing storehouse and goods a farmer might have brought as tithing payment. Example: Nine chicken eggs (or jelly beans) to the side for the farmer and one egg (or jelly bean) in the storehouse.

TITHING: I Want to Pay My Tithing
(tithing bills match game)

LESSON IDEAS: See lesson #42 in Primary 3-CTR B manual*.

YOU'LL NEED: Copy two sets of tithing bills (page 136) on colored cardstock paper for each child, scissors, and crayons

AGES 8-TEENS ACTIVITY: Create a tithing match to help child know that: (1) Tithing helps build temples and meetinghouses, (2) Tithing helps missionary work, (3) Tithing helps support family history and temple work, (4) Heavenly Father will bless us when we pay our tithing, and (5) I am happy to help by paying my tithing.

TO MAKE: Color and cut out tithing bills. For a larger family make two sets. **TO PLAY:** (1) Mix up and turn cards face down. (2) Take turns turning two cards over for others to see. (3) If a match is made, player collects the two matching cards. Player reads the card aloud to others, i.e. "Tithing helps missionary work." (4) Play until all cards are matched and read aloud.

THOUGHT TREAT: 10 Coin Cookies. Roll out sugar cookie dough and cut into quarter-size round shapes (use a cap from a 2-liter bottle to cut cookies). Paint with cookie paints. Bake about 6-8 minutes at 350°. To Make Cookie Paints: Mix two teaspoons canned milk with food coloring. Serve 10 to children, telling them to eat 9 and give one to the bishop.

*Primary manuals are published by The Church of Jesus Christ of Latter-day Saints, Salt Lake City, Utah.

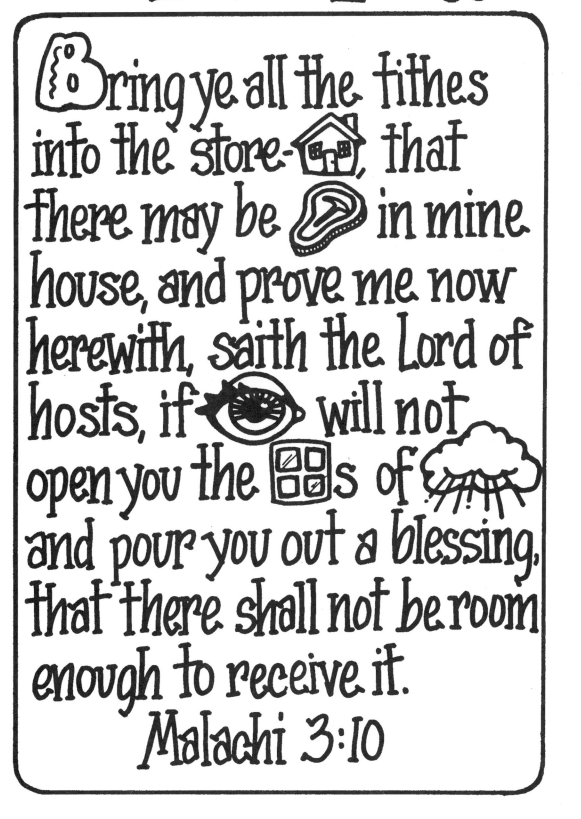

Bring ye all the tithes into the store-🏠, that there may be 🥩 in mine house, and prove me now herewith, saith the Lord of hosts, if 👁 will not open you the 🪟s of ☁ and pour you out a blessing, that there shall not be room enough to receive it.

Malachi 3:10

I earn a dime
My world is fine.
I pay a penny
My blessings are many!

I can pay
Tithing.

PATTERN: *TITHING (coins for tithing purse)*

A. - Fold in half with illustrations on the outside.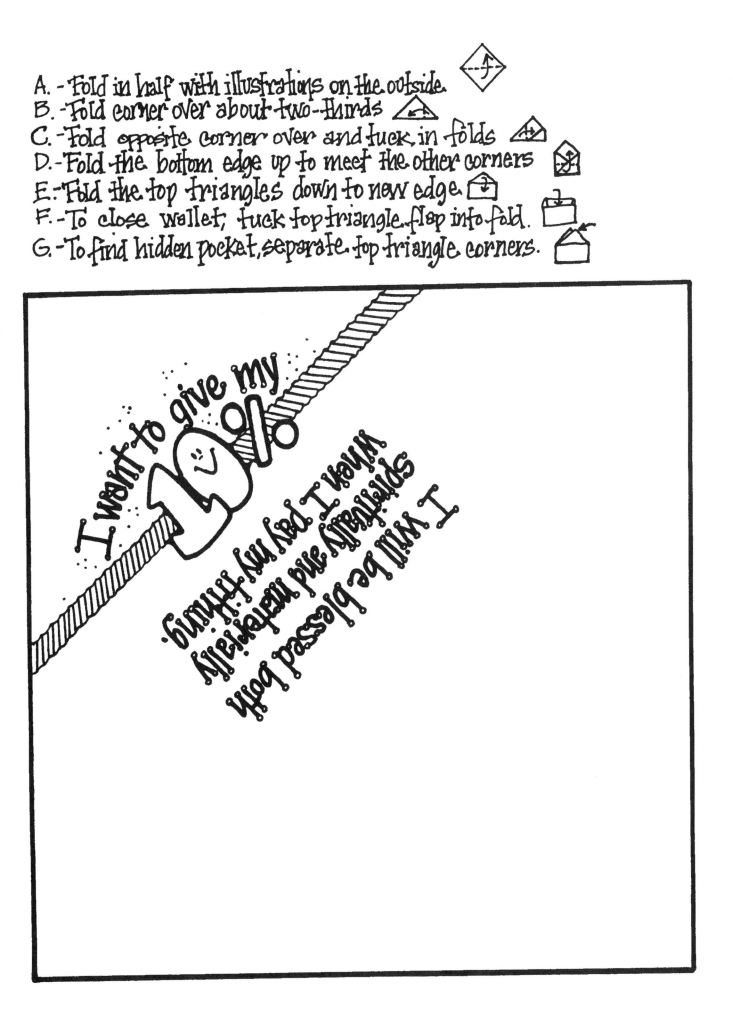
B. - Fold corner over about two-thirds
C. - Fold opposite corner over and tuck in folds
D. - Fold the bottom edge up to meet the other corners
E. - Fold the top triangles down to new edge.
F. - To close wallet, tuck top triangle flap into fold.
G. - To find hidden pocket, separate top triangle corners.

I want to give my 10%

when I pay my tithing.
spiritually and materially

I will be blessed both

PATTERN: *TITHING (tithing bills match game)*

WORD OF WISDOM: *I Will Obey This Great Law of Health*

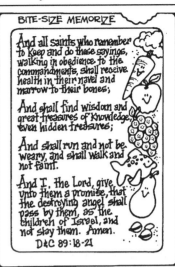

PREPARE AHEAD: Scripture Lesson, Bite-size Memorize Poster, Activity, and Thought Treat

OPENING SONG/PRAYER: "The Lord Gave Me a Temple," page 153 in the Children's Songbook*

BITE-SIZE MEMORIZE: Present the D&C 89:18-21 poster (shown right) on page 139. Color poster and display to learn.

SCRIPTURE LESSON: Search and ponder scriptures below.

WORD OF WISDOM: *I Will Obey This Great Law of Health*

THE WORD OF WISDOM asks us to abstain from (not use) alcohol,
tobacco, coffee, tea, and harmful drugs. . . . . .D&C 89:7-9
REWARD for keeping the Word of Wisdom (keeps body and spirit strong). . . . . D&C 89:18-21
Rewards for obedience to God's laws. . . . . Helaman 10:4-5, Mosiah 2:22, D&C 59:23
BLESSINGS COME FROM KEEPING THE LORD'S LAW OF HEALTH (eating good food).
Tell how Daniel and his brethren, Shadrach, Meshach, and Abed-nego, were blessed for
keeping the Lord's law of health (Daniel 1:4-21 and compare with D&C 89:7, 12).
Another story about Shadrach, Meshach, and Abed-nego is found in *Old Testament
Stories** "Shadrach, Meshach, and Abed-nego," pages 154-155 (Daniel 3).
WORD OF WISDOM THOUGHTS:
Our body is a temple. . . . . .1 Corinthians 3:16-17; 6:19-20
Be careful what you eat, and don't eat in excess. . . . . Deuteronomy 14:3, D&C 59:16-20
Avoid strong drink. . . . . Judges 13:13-14, Proverbs 20:1, Isaiah 5:11-12, Daniel 1
Give your body rest, but don't sleep more than needful. . . . . D&C 88:124, Exodus 20:9-10
Do not be a drunkard or glutton. . . . . .Proverbs 23:20-21
Do not labor beyond your strength. . . . . D&C 10:4
Eat meat sparingly. . . . . D&C 89:12
Obeying the Word of Wisdom shows we are willing to choose the right. . . . . .Moroni 7:16-17,
. . . . 2 Nephi 2:27-28, Alma 53:18-21, Deuteronomy 6:17-18, 1 Timothy 4:12

HOME-SPUN FUN ACTIVITIES: Select activities from the following pages to make learning fun.

CLOSING SONG/PRAYER: "The Word of Wisdom," page 154 in Children's Songbook*

THOUGHT TREAT: <u>Food Fun Picnic</u>. Spread out a blanket and serve healthy food. Before eating, have a child thank Heavenly Father for the good food and ask him to bless the food. If possible, have the child help prepare the food to make it more appealing.

MORE LESSON IDEAS: IDEA #1—*Gospel Principles** Chapter 29 (pages 192-195)
IDEA #2—Primary lessons found in the *Primary** manuals (see LESSON IDEAS, page 138)
IDEA #3—*Family Home Evening Resource Book** (pages 228-231)
IDEA #4—*Uniform System for Teaching the Gospel** missionary discussions #4 (pages 4-16, 17, 18)
IDEA #5—*Doctrine and Covenants Stories** "The Word of Wisdom," pages 119-122

WORD OF WISDOM *Activities and Lesson Ideas*

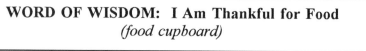

WORD OF WISDOM: I Am Thankful for Food
(food cupboard)

LESSON IDEAS: See lesson #32 in Primary 1 manual*.

YOU'LL NEED: Copy of food cupboard and food (page 140) on colored cardstock paper, scissors, glue, and crayons
AGES 3-7 ACTIVITY: Help children express their gratitude for good food as you place or glue food items in cupboard. FUN OPTION: Play a match game by copying two sets of food to match.

WORD OF WISDOM: I Am Blessed When I Eat Healthy
(Word of Wisdom Choices)

LESSON IDEAS: See lesson #14 in Primary 3-CTR B manual*.

YOU'LL NEED: Copy of Word of Wisdom Choices card and food pictures (pages 141-142) on colored cardstock paper and an 8 1/2" x 11" sheet of lightweight paper for each child, scissors, and crayons
AGES 4-10 ACTIVITY: Create a pocket card with two pockets. Pocket #1: Garbage can with pocket to place unhealthy foods, and Pocket #2: Mouth with pocket to place healthy foods. This activity will remind children that they are blessed with a healthy body when they follow the commandments given in the Word of Wisdom (Doctrine and Covenants 89). (1) Color and cut out card and food and substance pictures. (2) Cut slit in garbage can and mouth. (3) Create a pocket by gluing sides and bottom of the back 1/4" to an 8 1/2" x 11" sheet of paper leaving top open to hold food.

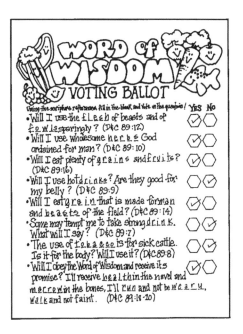

**WORD OF WISDOM: I Will Say "No"
to Harmful Things and "Yes" to Healthful**
(Word of Wisdom voting ballot)

LESSON IDEAS: See lesson #24 in Primary 5 manual*.

YOU'LL NEED: Copy of Word of Wisdom voting ballot (page 143) on colored cardstock paper, and a punch tack (to punch ballot) for each child, scissors, glue, and crayons
AGES 8-TEENS ACTIVITY: Help children vote "No" to harmful things for the body and "Yes" to healthful things. This voting process helps children decide to keep the Word of Wisdom revelation found in Doctrine and Covenants sections 88-89. (1) Color and cut out voting ballot. (2) Children read statement and vote "yes" or "no" by punching the column next to the statement. (3) Children can look up the scriptures and fill in the blank as they read the statements next to the scripture references.

*Primary manuals are published by The Church of Jesus Christ of Latter-day Saints, Salt Lake City, Utah.

And all saints who remember to keep and do these sayings, walking in obedience to the commandments, shall receive health in their navel and marrow to their bones;

And shall find wisdom and great treasures of knowledge, even hidden treasures;

And shall run and not be weary, and shall walk and not faint.

And I, the Lord, give unto them a promise, that the destroying angel shall pass by them, as the children of Israel, and not slay them. Amen.

D&C 89:18-21

I am thankful for FOOD!

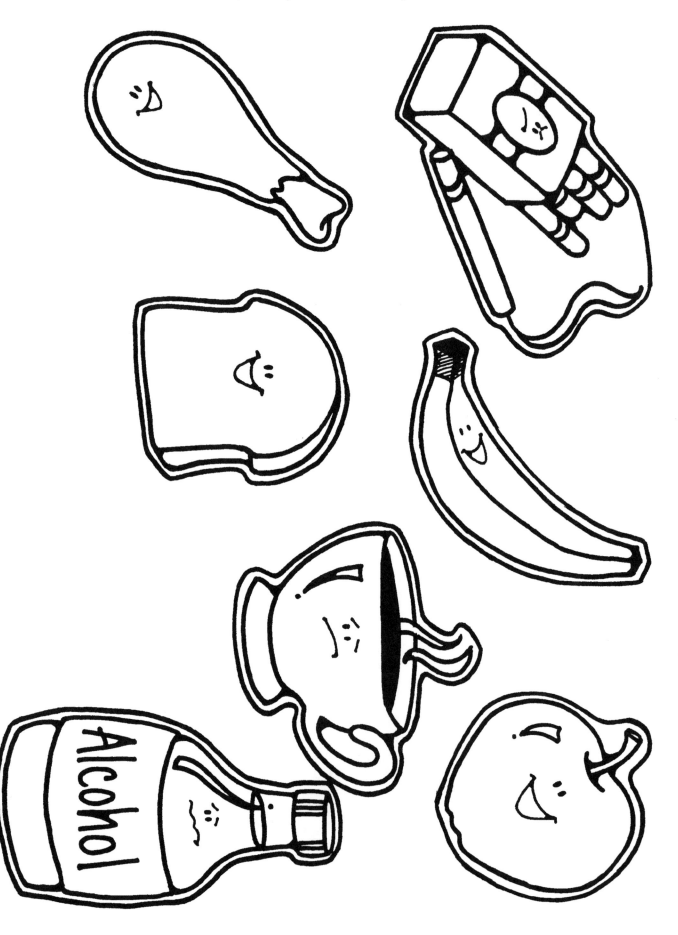

WORD of WISDOM
VOTING BALLOT

Using the scripture references, fill in the blank and vote on the questions!

YES   NO

• Will I use the _____ of beasts and of _____ sparingly? (D&C 89:12) ⬡ ⬡

• Will I use wholesome _____ God ordained for man? (D&C 89:10) ⬡ ⬡

• Will I eat plenty of _____s and _____s? (D&C 89:16) ⬡ ⬡

• Will I use hot _____? Are they good for my belly? (D&C 89:9) ⬡ ⬡

• Will I eat _____ that is made for _____ and _____ of the field? (D&C 89:14) ⬡ ⬡

• Some may tempt me to take strong _____. What will I say? (D&C 89:7) ⬡ ⬡

• The use of _____ is for sick cattle. Is it for the body? Will I use it? (D&C 89:8) ⬡ ⬡

• Will I obey the Word of Wisdom and receive its promise? I'll receive _____ in the navel and _____ in the bones, I'll _____ and not be _____, _____ and not faint. (D&C 89:18-20) ⬡ ⬡

Mary H. Ross, Author and
Jennette Guymon-King, Illustrator
are also the creators of:

PRIMARY PARTNERS:
A-Z Activities to Make Learning Fun for:
- Nursery and Age 3 (Sunbeams)
- CTR A & B Ages 4-7
- Book of Mormon Ages 8-11
- Doctrine & Covenants/Church History Ages 8-11
- Achievement Days, Girls Ages 8-11

MARY H. ROSS, Author

Mary Ross is an energetic mother, Primary teacher, and has been an Achievement Days leader. She loves to help children have a good time while they learn. She has studied acting and taught modeling and voice. Her varied interests include writing, creating activities and children's parties, and cooking. Mary and her husband, Paul, live with their daughter, Jennifer, in Sandy, Utah.

- Photos by Scott Hancock, Provo, Utah

JENNETTE GUYMON-KING,
Illustrator

Jennette Guymon-King has studied graphic arts and illustration at Utah Valley State College and the University of Utah. She is currently employed with a commercial construction company. She served a mission to Japan. Jennette enjoys sports, reading, cooking, art, gardening, and freelance illustrating. Jennette and her husband, Clayton, live in Riverton, Utah.

Opening Song
Scripture
Fun Song
Lesson /Story
Activity
Closing Song
Treat